Lives in Cricket: No 29

A.N.Hornby
The Boss

Stuart Brodkin

First published in Great Britain by
Association of Cricket Statisticians and Historians
Cardiff CF11 9XR.
© ACS, 2013

British Library Cataloguing-in-Publication Data.
A catalogue record for this book is available from the British Library.

ISBN: 978 1 908165 27 5
Typeset and printed by The City Press Leeds Ltd

Contents

'My Hornby and my Barlow long ago.' As befitted the attitudes of the age, the amateur (Hornby) is seated with a bat, while the professional (Barlow) stands and holds a ball.

Chapter One
The Ashes are born

Well, old fellow, it would have been the proudest moment of my life to have won but I cannot help congratulating you sincerely on the splendid uphill game and your well merited success – Hornby to the Australian captain Billy Murdoch

Captaining England on the second day of The Oval Test against Australia on 29 August, 1882, Albert Hornby must have thought he was well on the way to leading his side to victory. After all, England needed a mere 85 to win in their second innings and Hornby could be forgiven for thinking the match would not spill over into its third and final day.

Hornby was right – the third day wasn't required. But he was also wrong because it wasn't England who finished the game victorious, it was the Australians.

It appears the visitors were fired up by what they considered to be a piece of unsporting behaviour by the legendary W.G.Grace, who was as well known for his prowess as a cricketer as he was for his beard and win-at-all-costs attitude.

A grainy but evocative image of the 1882 Oval Test in progress.

Grace had controversially run out Australia No. 8 Sammy Jones. The incident happened when the visitors' captain Billy Murdoch hit the ball to leg and ran a single. Alfred Lyttelton, the wicket-keeper, followed the ball and threw it back to the stumps towards Ted Peate, who was at the wicket, but Peate missed it and it was gathered up by Grace, who was fielding at point. Grace held on to the ball for two or three seconds and Jones, assuming the ball was dead, moved out of his crease to do a bit of 'gardening'. It was at this point, with Jones out of his ground, that Grace walked up to the wicket and, taking off the bails, appealed to umpire Bob Thoms, who is alleged to have said: 'If you claim it, sir, it is out.'

Those words have gone down in history, but Charles Pardon, who was covering the tour for *Bell's Life* and who had heard what Thoms had allegedly said, spoke with Thoms and asked him what he actually said. Thoms told him that he had said all that was necessary in the circumstances, the single word 'out'.

Pardon reckoned that Jones was 'foolish' and that Grace 'did what he was perfectly justified in doing'. A.P. ('Bunny') Lucas, who also played in the match, later claimed that one of the Australians 'admitted he would have done the same thing if he had been where Grace was'. But there was a feeling that 'it wasn't cricket'. Certainly it had Spofforth seething – and, later in the day, that was to prove England's undoing.

Jones is also famous for helping to establish a cricketing superstition in his home country. His top Test score in twelve matches was 87 against England at Old Trafford in 1886. Ever since, that total – 13 short of a century – has been considered unlucky by Australians.

With Jones dismissed, Australia were 114 for seven, an overall lead of just 76. By now Spofforth had joined Murdoch, who hit Peate to the onside for three. But in the same over Peate did for Spofforth, bowling him middle stump, leaving Australia on 117 for eight. They were 79 ahead. Tom Garrett joined his captain and the latter managed a single and a two. Garrett then struck Hornby's Lancashire colleague Allan Steel very hard to the off, where Hornby was soon in hot pursuit of the ball. Garrett had taken two and called his partner for a third. But the Wollongong-born all-rounder had reckoned without Hornby's lightning fast reaction. The English captain threw the ball smartly to Studd, who returned it to Lyttelton, who broke the stumps in a flash. Murdoch was run out by about a yard and Australia were 122 for nine. Pardon was to describe this as 'the best bit of fielding in the match'. Australia No. 11 Harry Boyle was bowled first ball by Steel with no further addition to the score, leaving England to chase a very gettable target of 85 – and in cricketing terms they had almost all the time in the world to reach it.

Hornby, who had curiously batted at ten in the first innings, strode out with Grace to open England's second innings at quarter to four in the afternoon.

They started in circumspect fashion in their quest for the runs that would secure them victory. 'The moderate rate of run-getting,' said *The Times* report, 'was relieved by Mr Hornby driving a ball of Spofforth's to the on for four, while in the same over he made a lucky "snick" to leg for two. Two overs later, however, his off stump was struck, while [Dick] Barlow, who followed, had his wicket upset by the first ball he received.'

The *Manchester Evening News* reported in its first edition – in the days before radio's Test Match Special, Teletext, Cricinfo and rolling satellite sports news television programmes and when evening papers produced several editions each day – that by 4.45 pm, an hour after the innings had begun, the score was 40 for two, with England almost halfway to their modest target and with wickets in hand.

Fred 'The Demon' Spofforth, who, along with his colleagues, was so upset by the Jones run out incident that he told his team-mates shortly before England's openers took the field: 'This can be done,' had taken both England wickets.

Earlier, Spofforth was alleged to have visited the England dressing room and told Grace: 'You're a bloody cheat. This will lose you the match.' And Spofforth was true to his angry words. Bowling from the Vauxhall End with his arms flailing, he added five more scalps to his haul, ripping through the English ranks to claim seven for 44, giving the Australians an improbable seven-run victory.

Hornby was particularly gracious in defeat, telling the Australian captain Murdoch: 'Well, old fellow, it would have been the proudest moment of my life to have won but I cannot help congratulating you sincerely on the splendid uphill game and your well merited success.'

The Times correspondent reckoned Australia had the best of the wicket, which he claimed 'played very treacherously during the England innings'.

The 1882 Australian tourists.
Top: G.E.Palmer, H.F.Boyle, P.S.McDonnell, F.R.Spofforth, T.P.Horan, S.P.Jones.
Seated: W.L.Murdoch, G.Giffen, A.C.Bannerman, T.W.Garrett, H.H.Massie.

But the *Manchester Evening News* begged to differ, saying the wicket had proved equally difficult for both sides: 'These were the two best elevens in the world. It must be said, however, that on a wicket like that the best batsmen seem to do little better against good bowling than any moderate players.'

In suitably sombre mood the *Manchester Evening Mail* reported the grim news that at 13 minutes to six, just two hours and two minutes after England's openers Hornby and Grace had walked purposefully to the middle, the home side had succumbed, adding 'the game will long be remembered by those who had the good fortune to witness it'.

Indeed, it was such a tense finish that one spectator is reported to have died after bursting a blood vessel, while another allegedly chewed through his umbrella. Both these incidents sound apocryphal, but although the latter probably is the former almost certainly isn't.

As the *Manchester Evening Mail* stated on 30 August:

> Immediately after the conclusion of the match one of the spectators, named Spendler, who had journeyed from Eastbourne to be present, fell down, blood at the same time issuing from his mouth and nostrils.
> He was at once carried off the ground and examined by several medical men, amongst whom was Dr Jones, the president

of Surrey County Cricket Club. After a brief examination he was pronounced to have died from a congestion of the lungs accelerated by the bursting of a blood vessel.

Spofforth's match figures of fourteen for 90 were not bettered by an Australian until the unlikely figure of Bob Massie came along to take sixteen for 137 on his Test debut against England at Lord's 90 years later.

But was the Oval result such a surprise? It was a strong touring side and they won 24 of their 28 matches, beating all the major counties and were successful in two of their three fixtures against representative sides.

Despite presiding over the home side's loss, Hornby received the plaudits for his intelligent deployment of the England attack and his thoughtful field settings. *The Times* stated: 'Mr Hornby seemed to know the bowling which would most baffle the batsmen and varied it accordingly, while he altered the disposition of the field with great judgement.'

In fact, on the same day that England were crashing to defeat against the Australians, the *Manchester Evening News*, in a review of the Lancashire county season thus far, had this to say about Hornby: 'As captain he has discharged his duties with excellent judgement. He always plays up well and inspirits (sic) the team and to him in no small degree is owing our present position of supremacy.' At this stage of the season, Lancashire, under Hornby's stewardship, had won seven of their eight fixtures. The 'half-term report' also referred to Hornby's 'brilliant and certain fielding [that] sets an example which all endeavour to emulate but none surpass'.

But despite praise for Hornby's captaincy skills and his ability and agility in the field, Charles Pardon, who covered the Australian tour for *Bell's Life* and whose writings were later re-published in book form as *Australians in England*, felt that Hornby 'was not quite good enough to be in the [England] eleven'. 'I cannot see what form he has ever shown against Australian bowling in this country to justify his selection,' Pardon added rather caustically. But he did say that Hornby had taken part in 'the best bit of fielding in the match' when the English captain teamed up with Charles Studd and wicket-keeper Lyttelton to run out Murdoch, who was attempting a third run.

Hornby also drew praise from Australia's County Cork-born

all-rounder Tom Horan for keeping the Lancashire side in the field despite falling rain, as Australia made the 30 runs they needed for victory against Lancashire at Old Trafford in the twenty-first game of their tour in June of that year. Horan wrote:

> Luckily, the rain did not prevent the match being finished, but it is only fair to say that while the last 30 runs were being made it was raining in a manner that has often caused the field to be cleared in Melbourne and Sydney. Mr Hornby, however, with the true spirit of a sportsman and a gentleman, kept his men in the field, and afterwards admitted that the best team won.

But despite Horan's assertion that Hornby wasn't good enough to be in the side, Hornby still wouldn't have expected the reaction of some of the English media to England's defeat. The fallout led to one of his lasting legacies to cricket and it came in the shape of a diminutive urn.

It is part of cricketing folklore that the *Sporting Times'* mock obituary, published on 2 September, gave rise to the foundation of the Ashes. Written by Reginald Brooks, under the pseudonym 'Bloobs', it read: 'In affectionate remembrance of English cricket which died at The Oval, 29th August, 1882. Deeply lamented by a large circle of sorrowing friends and acquaintants, RIP. NB The body will be cremated and the Ashes taken to Australia.'

There were echoes of those sentiments almost exactly 129 years later – in August 2011 – when the *Times of India* mournfully acknowledged India's fall from top spot in the ICC Test world rankings after going 3-0 down in the four-match series against England with these words: 'RIP the world's No. 1 Test team.' India, beaten by an innings at Edgbaston, had held the No.1 position since 6 December 2009.

But, back in 1882, the *Sporting Times* wasn't the first in the field. Two days earlier, in the 31 August edition of *Cricket: A Weekly Record of the Game*, there was a similar outpouring of grief over the state of English cricket. Edited by Charles Alcock, the man who created the FA Cup in his guise as secretary of the Football Association, the publication produced the following 'death notice': 'Sacred to the memory of England's supremacy in the cricket-field which expired on the 29th day of August at The Oval. Its end was Peate.'

Even *Punch* got in on the act with this poem which it printed in its

9 September issue:

> Well done, Cornstalks! Whipt us
> Fair and square,
> Was it luck that tript us?
> Was it scare?
> Kangaroo Land's "Demon", or our own
> Want of "devil", coolness, nerve, backbone?

The final sentence of Alcock's lamentation was a reference to Ted Peate, the England slow left-armer and No. 11, who came to the crease with England needing just ten runs for victory. Peate succumbed for only two and the match was lost.

He arrived back in the dressing-room to be admonished for not having left the job of scoring the vital runs needed for victory to his partner, Studd. Rather perversely Peate explained: 'Ah weren't afeard for mesen. Ah were afeard for Meester Studd. Ah knew Ah could play old Spoff.'

Nearly fifty years later, Rev Robert Hindle reminisced in a letter to *The Times*: 'It was said that Mr Studd sat [in the committee room before going out to bat] with three sweaters on and shook with nervousness. As a result Mr Hornby kept him back with the result that all the wickets were down before Mr Studd received a ball, and the match was lost by seven runs.'

Charles Thomas Studd was certainly not a rabbit and had batted at No. 6 in the first innings where he was bowled third ball by Spofforth for nought. But notwithstanding that failure he was fairly reliable with the bat. He played in five Tests for his country, averaging 20 with a highest score of 48 and appeared 34 times for Middlesex where his average rose to 28.20 with one century and four fifties.

In 1926, Studd had told Rev Hindle, rather defensively it might be thought: 'I see from a newspaper that they now declare that I asked Hornby not to let me go in. Of course, that is without the shadow of a foundation in fact. The only truth of the whole matter as stated is that the weather was cold and we sat in the committee room with the windows closed because of the cold.'

Studd added:

> Hornby, on his own account, began to alter the order of going in. I believe he did ask me if I minded, and I said 'no'. Then things began to change and the procession began. Hornby told

me he was holding me in reserve.
So I went in eighth man and saw two wickets fall, but I never received a ball. Now here are the facts. Nobody dreamed, half an hour before the finish, that we could be beaten. Fifty odd out of seventy had been made and eight men still to go in.
What reason could there be for my nerves being bad as stated by Hornby? Again, if Hornby believed me to be nervous he should have put me in first. This is what is usually done.

Studd's recollection of events at The Oval has not stood the test of time. He, in fact, batted at No. 10 and not No. 8 as he stated and he did face a couple of deliveries, neither of which he managed to score from. England, of course, required 85 for victory and not seventy as Studd had written.

Whatever the truth of Hornby's shuffling of the batting pack, there is no doubt that it was mainly thanks to Charles Alcock and the *Sporting Times* that from that day hence England and Australia would compete for the Ashes.

C.T.Studd, whose role in the final stages of the
1882 Oval Test remains controversial. He later gave up cricket
to become a missionary in China, Africa and India.

Initially, though, the Ashes were referred to half-jokingly when Ivo Bligh toured Australia in 1882/83 and the Australian media caught on to the term. But in the 20 years following Bligh's tour, which resulted in a 2-1 Test series win for England, the term largely disappeared from the cricketing lexicon – in both Australia and England.

However, the concept of the Ashes was resuscitated when Australian all-rounder George Giffen, in his memoirs, *With Bat and Ball*, published in 1898, used the term as if it were well known to all.

It gained its real renaissance when Pelham Warner took a team Down Under in 1903 and vowed to regain the Ashes. The Australian media wasn't slow to latch on to the concept and this time it stuck. Having fulfilled his promise to win back the mythical Ashes, Warner published *How We Recovered the Ashes* in 1905 although strangely enough the origins of the term are not referred to in the text. *Wisden's Cricketers' Almanack* caught up with the term in the same year.

Hornby's elevation to the England captaincy came after 15 seasons of first-class cricket and three years after his only previous Test appearance in the ten-wicket defeat by Australia in Melbourne in January 1879.

Two days before the Kennington Oval epic, Hornby had featured in Lancashire's home game against Middlesex. Hornby captained the side to victory by an innings and 271 runs. The first day's play was abandoned through rain. Hornby made only 11 with Lancashire's top scorer Walter Robinson hitting 101. Hornby must have travelled down to London with his county colleague Dick Barlow on the Sunday. They were joined in the Test side by another Lancashire man, Allan Steel, who played in only seven first-class matches for Lancashire in that season, whereas Hornby and Barlow played in 20 each.

Hornby was to play only one further Test, in 1884, also against Australia at Old Trafford, a match which ended in a draw after rain washed out the first day of the three-day fixture. Once again, he captained the side. Thus his record as England captain was poor – one defeat and a draw in his two matches in charge.

In all, in his three Test appearances, Hornby failed to do himself justice with the bat, scoring two and four in Melbourne, two and nine at The Oval and nought and four in front of his own supporters at Old Trafford, a miserable total of 21 runs for an equally miserable average of 3.5.

The Oval Test that begat the Ashes was at the midpoint of Hornby's lengthy playing career, but, outwardly, it didn't seem to affect him in any noticeable way.

In fact, Hornby, captaining a rather depleted North of England against the auld enemy (Australia) at Old Trafford a fortnight later, was to gain some measure of compensation with a comprehensive win. Without the services of Steel, Billy Barnes and Fred Morley, who were en route to Australia, and Arthur Shrewsbury, whose finger was too sore to allow him to take part, the North still proved more than a match for the Aussies. The North needed only 28 for victory in their second innings and there must have been a good deal of satisfaction for Hornby, batting with his Lancashire opening partner Barlow, as he struck two fours in an over off the bowling of Tom Garrett and cut a ball from his nemesis, Spofforth, 'grandly behind point for four thus finishing the game'. The North reached their target in 8.3 overs with Hornby unbeaten on 18 and Barlow not out 11 as they romped to a ten-wicket win. Pardon, in his book *Australians in England*, may have been over-egging the pudding, but he declared very firmly: 'There was no luck and no fluke about the match, which was to a considerable extent revenge for the Oval defeat of August 29, and supports the opinion I have always held that, strong as the Australians are, they are not equal to our very best teams when the ground is in good order.' Obviously another fan of Hornby's leadership skills, Pardon added: 'It is necessary to mention the admirable judgement displayed by Hornby in placing his field and changing his bowling.'

The *Stockport Advertiser* wasn't slow in comparing this win to England's defeat at The Oval. Their report stated:

> When the Colonists came off the victors in the match played against the representative English team at Kennington Oval one might have imagined – judging from the mournful wailings of some of the organs in the Press – that British supremacy in cricket had been removed once and for ever.
> The result of the more recent contest at Old Trafford dispels the ludicrous fallacy, and proves clearly that matches of an international character should not be decided by a single game, subject as it is to the tricks of atmosphere and fortune. Brilliant cricket was shown on both sides during each of the

three days at Manchester and the performance of both teams are eminently worthy of the warmest praise.

Mr Hornby, as captain of the Northmen, succeeded admirably.

After that fateful Oval Test, Hornby's playing career was a remarkably long one. He went on for a another 17 years until 1899 and might have stretched that even further, but was forced to pull out of what would have been his final first-class match for an England XI against the West Indians at Whitegate Park, Blackpool on 26 July, 1906, suffering from lumbago. He was replaced by Albert Peatfield, who was playing his only first-class game at the age of 32. Peatfield had, in fact, played for Glamorgan in 1903 in matches which were not considered first-class.

So Hornby's bid to sign off from first-class cricket in a relatively high-profile game was aborted almost exactly six years after his previous appearance in a major match – for Lancashire, also against West Indies, at Old Trafford in July 1900. Hornby didn't exactly bow out in a blaze of glory in that game, scoring four in the first innings and being absent for Lancashire's second knock in the home side's 57-run win against the tourists who included Lebrun Constantine, father of the great Learie Constantine, later Sir Learie.

Hornby had played his last Championship match in the previous season at the age of 52 – the oldest-ever Lancashire player in that competition – in the same side as his son, Albert Henry. Typically, Hornby excelled in that final, competitive fixture, scoring 53 out of a stand of 63 for the eighth wicket in 65 minutes.

But although his final game against the West Indian tourists was a bit of an anti-climax, Hornby's cricketing career was, for the most part, extremely successful. He later enjoyed similar success in his capacity as chairman and president of the club.

Chapter Two

Born with a silver spoon

He is a most brilliant and punishing hitter, his scores in the great contests of the day being very large – Scores and Biographies on Hornby

The Hornby family

Hornby's cricketing, indeed his sporting curriculum vitae, was outstanding, but he did get off to a rather good start in life. Albert Neilson Hornby was born in Blackburn on 10 February, 1847, the sixth son of William Henry Hornby. He probably took his middle name from Robert Neilson, a fellow-magistrate of his father's. Hornby senior was the founder of W.H.Hornby & Co., cotton spinners and manufacturers, who provided work for about 1,400 people at Brookhouse Mill, one of four major mills in Hornby's home town. Hornby & Co.'s competitors were William Eccles & Co, Robert Hopwood & Sons, and Pilkington, Brother & Co.

The source of the Hornby family prosperity:
Brookhouse Mill with its glory days long since gone.

In addition to his cotton manufacturing business, Albert's father founded Sunday schools in conjunction with St Michael's Church in Derrikens in Brookhouse in April 1840 and was a governor of Blackburn Grammar School.

He was also a leading promoter – and chairman – of the railway that ran between his home town and Bolton and Clitheroe. When that company was amalgamated with the Lancashire & Yorkshire Railway he became a director of the latter. William was the town's first mayor, being elected in November 1851 and the following March was presented 'by a number of the burgesses and other inhabitants' with a gold chain and civic badge. He was also supportive of the first important measure for regulating the hours worked in factories, known as the Ten Hours Bill. Presumably as a mark of appreciation for his efforts, the workforce at Brookhouse Mill presented him with 'an address and silver vase'.

Young Hornby first saw the light of day at Brook House, in King Street, Blackburn. It was a rather grandiose mansion, but in design almost as utilitarian as the mill.

After failing in the by-election of 1853, he was elected as Conservative MP for Blackburn in the General Election of March 1857, retaining his seat in the subsequent General Elections of 1859 and 1865. In 1863 he made his only speech in the House of Commons, in response to William Ferrand MP, who had attacked the cotton manufacturing industry.

But William was never far away from controversy in the political arena. He retained his seat for a third time in November 1868, together with his kinsman Joseph Feilden, but the pair were accused of intimidating voters. A petition was heard at the town hall in March 1869 by Mr Justice Willes as a result of which the election was declared void. In the wake of Justice Willes' ruling, William quietly returned to private life, but at the resulting by-election his son Edward was elected along with Joseph's son Henry Master Feilden. Both candidates appealed for support as a tribute to their fathers, and Edward Hornby asserted that he had 'no vain idea' that his own merits were enough to qualify him as an MP.

In another political incident many years earlier, during the election of 1835, William was thrown over the parapet of Salford bridge in Blackburn by an infuriated mob, but escaped unhurt. He had just emerged from the Bay Horse Inn with a few friends when he was set upon and thrown into the mud on the easterly side of the stream that ran beneath the bridge. Charles Haworth, a well-known local artist, who was an eye-witness, helped to scrape the mud from William's clothes in a hat shop on the bridge. Aged only 27, he had become chairman of the Blackburn Conservative party when the town was given two MPs under the Reform Act of 1832.

A.N.'s father, William Henry Hornby, cotton manufacturer, employer of 1,400 people, first Mayor of Blackburn and the town's MP for twelve years. The portrait is a detail from 'The Laying of the Foundation Stone of the Blackburn Cotton Exchange', painted by Vladimir Ossipovich Sherwood in 1863.

A fine athlete in his day, William was known affectionately as 'Th'Owd Game Cock'. He had the reputation of being a somewhat prickly customer, a man who would never shy away from a fight, and, clearly, Albert inherited a great deal of his father's combative nature.

On 18 July 1912 a statue to William Henry Hornby was unveiled by his son Sir Harry, at Limbrick overlooking Sudell Cross in the town. It is a fine statue in bronze with the bewhiskered Hornby, wearing a bow tie and a long waistcoat and overcoat and leaning gently on his walking stick, looking down in rather fatherly manner on the town's inhabitants just as he may have done in his heyday. In 1970 the statue was moved, minus its original ornate plinth, to a more central location close to the town hall, and is still there to this day.

Unveiling ceremony for a statue to W.H.Hornby in 1912.

Although very much a hard-headed businessman, William was seen as a model employer of his day and was respected by the majority of his workforce. He also earned the rather grudging respect of his political opponents. He died at the age of 79 in September 1884.

A.N. didn't follow his father into politics although in 1904 there was speculation that he might stand as MP for Blackburn when Sir

Harry Hornby and Sir William Coddington were expected to retire. But A.N. wasn't prepared to accept the nomination, and in fact Sir Harry stood again.

Apart from our subject, William had six other sons, one of whom died young, and four daughters. The Hornby family was wealthy enough to be able to send all but one of the surviving boys to Harrow.

The eldest, **John (1838-1901)**, went on to Trinity College, Cambridge, and became a barrister. He was the only one not to have played cricket at a fairly high level.

Edward Kenworthy (1839-87) played his cricket with Cheshire from 1861-78. He entered the family business and followed his father as MP for Blackburn (1869-74).

William Henry junior (1841-1928) was known as Harry. He was educated privately and thus the only one of the brothers not to attend Harrow. He also joined the family business and became MP for Blackburn (1886-1910), but in 24 years made one intervention fewer than his father, never attempting to speak in the House. He was created Baron Hornby of Brookhouse, St. Michael, Blackburn in 1899.

A.N.'s brother, Sir William Henry (Harry) Hornby, as Conservative Parliamentary Candidate for Blackburn in 1905. The election of Labour's Philip Snowden to the two-member constituency, alongside Hornby, marked the beginning of a shift in the political allegiance of the town, which was completed after 1945 when first Barbara Castle then Jack Straw made it a Labour stronghold.

Harry played his cricket for Cheshire (1861-63), and was the joint-founder and first captain of the East Lancashire Cricket Club.

Cecil Lumsden (1843-96) played in one match for Lancashire (1877) and also appeared for Cheshire between 1861 and 1874. He joined the Army and retired as a captain in 1881, having served in the Zulu War of 1879 and the first Boer War in 1880-81. When in September 1876 he was called away on military duty, A.N. stepped in and played for Eighteen of Chichester against James Lillywhite's Australian tourists at Priory Park Ground, shortly before their return to Australia.

Charles Herbert (1849-93) went to Harrow, played cricket for Cheshire (1863-76) and married well – clearly, all Hornby traits!

In 1856 the Hornbys moved to Shrewbridge Hall at Nantwich in Cheshire, where in 1861 eight of the children were with them and they had no fewer than 15 servants. They left around 1867 and the hall was purchased in 1883 by the Nantwich Salt Springs Hotel Ltd and re-opened in 1893 as the Brine Baths Hotel. As Nantwich sought to establish itself as a spa town, the hotel became known for the healing properties of its natural salt water and springs, and was said to cure rheumatism, fits and other complaints. There were facilities for permanent residents, for visitors undergoing hydrotherapy and for the Cheshire Hunt, with suites reserved during the hunting season and stabling for 50 horses. The hotel was later sold and turned into a convalescent home for miners and was eventually demolished in 1958. Now only the brine baths, installed in 1892, remain as a reminder of the once thriving salt trade. Ironically, A.N.Hornby suffered greatly from rheumatism in his later years.

In 1871 the parents and two of their offspring were living at Poole Hall near Nantwich, but A.N. and his older brothers E.K. and W.H. were back in Blackburn in a separate household at Brookhouse Cottage, Whalley Road, in the heart of the area where the mill was situated. All three were described as 'cotton spinning manufacturers', so perhaps their 65-year-old father had more or less retired and they were running the family business, although A.N. was not to be involved with it for long.

You might think that Hornby Lodge in Bury New Road, Prestwich, Greater Manchester, might have once been the home of the Hornby cricketing family. In fact, it was the family domicile of the Hornby train set family. Hornby is quite a common name in Lancashire, and William Henry's cotton firm had no connection with the model railway manufacturers. Hornby Lodge was built in 1900 and later became offices and then a rather grand police station in its own wooded grounds. In 2002 it was sold by Greater Manchester Police to developers who built luxury apartments on the site, retaining the name Hornby Lodge.

The young cricketer

When the Hornby family moved to Nantwich, the five cricketing brothers became qualified for Cheshire by residence. In August 1862, aged barely 15½, A.N. played for Ludlow against a Gentlemen of Cheshire side containing no fewer than three of his brothers – Cecil Lumsden, Edward Kenworthy and William Henry. It was a chastening experience for the young man. E.K. scored 134 in the Gentlemen of Cheshire's mammoth total of 517 all out and Ludlow could only manage totals of 90 and 165 in reply, going under by an innings and 262 runs.

In Cheshire's innings, opening bat William Armitstead scored 177. He had earlier become famous for the introduction of white coats for umpires following the Free Foresters' game against a United England XI at G.P.Codic's Ground at Eccles, Manchester in the previous year. Rather like Hornby, he had two brothers in the opposition. One of them, John Richard, was later to officiate at Hornby's wedding.

A.N.'s contribution was only five and 21 but evidently he impressed his opponents, because Cheshire invited him to play for them three days later. He appeared for them in non-first-class cricket 23 times between then and 1876, scoring 1,672 runs at an average of 52.25, and taking 39 wickets. His highest score was 201 for the Gentlemen of Cheshire against the Gentlemen of Shropshire at the County Ground, Frankwell in Shrewsbury in 1868.

In August 1866, Hornby played for the Gentlemen of Cheshire against the Gentlemen of Lancashire at Chelford, scoring 38 and six, and taking a wicket and two catches. Three weeks later he had switched sides and was representing the Gentlemen of Lancashire against the Gentlemen of Yorkshire at York, scoring 13 and eight.

Hornby had begun his cricketing journey in 1862 at Harrow. There in 1864 and 1865 he was coached by the Earl of Bessborough, better known as Frederick Ponsonby, who devoted many years to Harrow cricket after playing 67 first-class matches. He was a member of the Harrow cricket eleven in both years, playing against Eton at Lord's a fortnight before W.G.Grace first graced the hallowed turf.

He opened the batting on each occasion, scoring 19 and 27 in the two games, both of which Harrow won by an innings.

At that time Hornby was 5ft 3in and is said to have weighed a mere 6st 'bat and all'. His schoolmates nicknamed him 'Monkey' because of his diminutive stature and boundless energy. Although in later years he grew to about 5ft 7in, which was average height for the time, his soubriquet remained with him for the rest of his life.

Hornby spent a brief period at Oxford University, but wasn't cut out to be an academic – he preferred scorebooks to textbooks – and soon returned to the family business. It was said that the family was relieved that Hornby, uninterested in a business career, didn't stay at Brookhouse Mill for long.

It is surprising that Hornby played for the Gentlemen of England against Oxford and Cambridge Universities Past and Present at Kennington Oval in June 1874, as Hornby's team was supposed to be selected from those 'who had not been educated at the Universities', whereas Hornby had spent a short time at Oxford. Presumably, Hornby's short stint in the city of dreaming spires didn't qualify as an education.

In Volume Eight of Frederick Lillywhite's *Scores and Biographies*, Arthur Haygarth painted this picture of the emerging Hornby:

> Few cricketers have appeared on the 'tented field' that are more distinguished than the subject of this notice.
> He is a most brilliant and punishing hitter, his scores in the great contests of the day being very large. His fielding is magnificent, generally taking long leg or cover point and though a right-hand bat he bowls right and left, using both hands (though he does not excel in this department of the game), being an ambidexter [sic].
> His style is beautiful and his forward play grand, getting well over the ball.

The East Lancashire Cricket Club

It was in his post-Harrovian days, that Hornby honed his skills playing for East Lancashire, a Blackburn-based club which was established as a private venture for the benefit of the officers of the 2nd East Lancashire Volunteers Regiment and members of the gentry. The Hornbys most definitely belonged to this latter level of society and Albert's father donated £500 – probably more than

£20,000 in 2012 values – towards the laying out of the ground at Alexandra Meadows, which had previously been in use as the regiment's parade ground. The ground was named to mark the wedding of Princess Alexandra of Denmark, who married Albert Edward, Prince of Wales, on 10 March 1863, becoming Princess of Wales. It was ready for use by the summer of 1864.

Cricket had been played in Blackburn at least as early as 1831, when Blackburn Cricket Club played Preston on a field near The Fox and Grapes public house. By 1849, the club had moved to Daisyfield, where East Lancashire were later to play their first match.

East Lancashire challenged the Blackburn club to a match at Daisyfield on 3 July, 1863 [some reports suggest the match was played on 23 July]. The new club proved popular with the locals and attracted around 200 members, soon appointing its first groundsman, William Lucas, on a wage of 18 shillings (roughly the equivalent of £40 in 2013) per week. Things were moving apace and there were already two professionals, Luke Greenwood and Joseph Kaye, both from across the Pennines in Yorkshire. Greenwood played more than 50 games for Yorkshire, and captained them in 1874. A new professional, John Smith, appeared on the scene in 1864. He was paid £2 10s (£110) a week, but results were only moderate.

Prior to the formation of the Lancashire Cricket League in March 1892 friendlies were played against teams like Preston, Great Harwood, Cheetham Hill, Church, Bolton, Burnley, Stonyhurst and Clayton-le-Moors.

Hornby was showing some promise at a decent level, and eventually made his debut for East Lancashire at Burnley on 10 June, 1867. He opened the batting in East Lancashire's first innings and carried his bat for nine not out in a total of 17; in the second innings he was again undefeated, making 20 out of 56.

Four Hornbys played for East Lancashire against Preston, helping the side to an innings victory. A.N. scored 56, C.L. made 33, E.K. contributed 15 and W.H. just managed to reach double figures, scoring ten.

In 1870 Hornby scored his second double hundred, this time an unbeaten 214 for East Lancashire against Accrington. It was in that game that East Lancashire amassed a mammoth 423 for six, but they took so long to reach that total that they left their opponents no time for a reply! In minor matches, Hornby compiled a further eight centuries.

But Hornby's appearances for East Lancashire were becoming rarer and rarer as Lancashire began calling on his services. Even though not a regular playing member at Alexandra Meadows, he was still instrumental in organising friendlies for the club and in 1886 he was elected a life member.

In August 1879, Hornby was part of a Lancashire XI that took on Eighteen of East Lancashire in a benefit for James Shaw, who played ten seasons as a professional for East Lancashire. In a 21-year career, Shaw also played for Nottinghamshire and no fewer than 30 other teams, including An England XI, R.Daft's XI and Christ Church, Oxford. On a ground that meant so much to him, A.N. would have wanted to do well, but he managed only one and three and to add further ignominy, a relatively strong Lancashire XI subsided to an eleven-wicket defeat. The fixture was repeated in the following year when the county side had rather the better of a draw, Hornby contributing 21 and 21 not out.

The Lancashire team that drew with the East Lancashire Club in 1880. Standing (l to r), J.F.Armistead, C.A.G.Hulton, A.Appleby, A.Watson, G.Nash. Seated: R.Pilling, W.Robinson, E.B.Rowley, A.N.Hornby, Rev.V.P.F.A. Royle, O.P.Lancashire. On the ground: R.G.Barlow. James Fisher Armistead was a Blackburn landowner and JP, unrelated to the Armitstead brothers who played cricket with and against Hornby. Part of the Alexandra Meadows ground can be glimpsed in the background.

Fifty-two years later Alexandra Meadows staged a Championship match when Lancashire broke new ground by playing there in May 1932 with Glamorgan providing the opposition. But the weather gods were unkind to say the least. It began raining at tea time on the first day and continued for the next two days. Glamorgan paid another visit to Alexandra Meadows three years later and they again brought the rain with them: only five and three-quarter hours play were possible on the first two days and none at all on the third and final day with the match being drawn. In between those two fixtures against the Welsh county, Lancashire managed innings victories over Worcestershire (1933) and Northamptonshire (1934). The Lancashire committee decided to wash their hands of Blackburn as a Championship venue and the fixture allocated to it for 1936 was switched to Preston.

No further Championship games have been played in Blackburn although 21 second eleven fixtures were staged at Alexandra Meadows, the last of them in 1985.

The East Lancashire club continues to thrive and has, in more recent times, attracted professionals of the calibre of Test players like Pakistan's Fazal Mahmood and Australians Allan Border and Paul Reiffel. And the Hornby family's legacy at the club, which still plays at Alexandra Meadows, lives on. After refurbishment in the 1990s, the new bar area was named the Hornby Lounge.

The Alexandra Meadows ground in November 2012.

Starting out for Lancashire

In June 1867, Hornby – at the age of 20 – made his debut for Lancashire against Yorkshire in the first Roses match ever played. The game, which has subsequently been granted official status, was staged at the picturesque Station Road Ground, at Whalley in the Ribble Valley. It is the only first-class fixture to have been played at the Whalley Cricket Club, but the club did provide

Lancashire with its most successful captain: Leonard Green skippered the side from 1926 to 1928 – and in all three seasons they won the County Championship.

But although it was the end of the first-class line for Station Road, it was the start of a 32-year playing association with the Red Rose county for Hornby.

However, it proved to be an inauspicious beginning for the youngster. He opened the batting in the first innings, scoring two, and batted at No. 5 when Lancashire followed on, bettering that score by just a single run as the home side, bowled out for 57 and 75, went down to a heavy defeat by an innings and 56 runs.

But Hornby, who was dismissed in both innings by George Freeman (12 for 51 in the match), did manage to hang on to a catch in Yorkshire's innings helping to send back the Yorkshire opener Joseph Rowbotham for seven. It was young Hornby's only Lancashire appearance of the season.

A week later, the two sides met again in Lancashire, at Old Trafford. Once more, Yorkshire inflicted another heavy defeat on their cross-Penninc rivals, winning by 165 runs. The sides met for a third time in Lancashire's final first-class match of a six-game season in September. This time the venue was the inelegantly named Swatter's Carr, Linthorpe Road East Ground in Middlesbrough. It was the second – and final – time the ground had staged first-class cricket. The only other first-class fixture played there had been three years earlier when Yorkshire entertained Kent. The Middlesbrough public saw Yorkshire coast to another easy win over the visitors with Lancashire going under by an innings and 40 runs to complete a hat-trick of defeats. It was a loss that was typical of a disastrous season for Lancashire, who lost four games and drew the other two.

A year after his Lancashire debut, in a match starting on 29 June 1868, Hornby turned in a remarkable all-round performance for the Eleven Gentlemen of East Lancashire against the Australian Aboriginal Eleven at Alexandra Meadows. He took four for 39 in the Australian first innings and six for 41 in their second and scored 117 runs opening the batting. The match ended in a disputed draw with the East Lancashire side on six for one, needing just two runs to win with nine wickets in hand.

It was the twelfth match of an extremely arduous tour for the Aboriginals, who played their first game against the Surrey Club at

Kennington Oval on 25 May and took the field for the 47th and final time as late as 17 October. There was a certain symmetry about their tour finale as that was also at Kennington Oval – against Gentlemen of Surrey – where it all began almost five months earlier. They took part in 36 two-day games and eleven fixtures scheduled for three days. Along the way the Aboriginals played a variety of sides, including the MCC (at Lord's), the Gentlemen of Lewisham, the Gentlemen of Rochdale, Blackheath, Bootle, Bishop's Stortford, Longsight, Richmond and Middlesbrough. They also played against the Sporting Press at Mote Park, Maidstone.

In his second season for Lancashire, in 1868, Hornby played his second match for the county, opening the batting in the final match of the season in what was his first appearance at Old Trafford. He scored eight and seven in another Lancashire defeat.

However, in 1869 he devoted far more time to cricket and played in three of Lancashire's four matches, scoring six and 61 in the county's defeat of Sussex at Old Trafford, and 18 and 42 in a win against Surrey. It was probably these performances that earned him selection on 28 June for the Gentlemen against the Players at Lord's in the second of the two fixtures between the sides played in that season. In the days before Test matches, recognition in this series was the highest honour in the game, although he scored only eight and two.

But although he gave more of himself to Lancashire, only one of the games was away from home. The club captain Edmund Rowley wasn't satisfied. He felt that the amateurs in the side were not playing in enough fixtures away from their Manchester headquarters.

In August of the 1869 season, Rowley was moved to write a letter to Arthur Appleby, who at the time was probably the best amateur bowler in England:

> When Lancashire have such men in the county as yourself and Hornby and they will not play, I think it is only fair to expect that the matches will be lost.
> At the commencement of the season I was very glad to hear that you and Hornby had arranged to play with Lancashire in all the County matches and I certainly understood that Lancashire was to have the preference – but may I ask has this arrangement been kept?
> My own idea is that County Cricket is the best that can be played and I really think that you should throw over any engagement

you may have for the sake of playing for your county.

Later in the letter, Rowley added: 'When I am getting up the team to play against Zingari on the 27th and 28th of August you will personally oblige me if you will play on those days. With your aid I think we shall be able to give the swells a good licking.' Rowley wrote a similar letter to Hornby.

Rowley was talking about picking the Manchester team (in effect the Lancashire 2nd XI) to play I Zingari at Old Trafford on those dates. Appleby did play although Hornby wasn't available. Manchester didn't, in the event, give the swells a good licking, but they did have the better of a rain-ruined match. In fact, Rowley didn't set a particularly good example to the stay-at-home amateurs himself, playing in only seven of the county's first 26 away matches, while his brother Alexander played ten of his 12 matches at home. Hornby's record was not good, either. He played in only six of a possible 23 away games after his debut at Whalley.

By 1870 Hornby may well have taken Rowley's letter to heart as he played in all four Lancashire first-class matches, two of them away fixtures, and scored his initial first-class century, 132 against Hampshire at Old Trafford on the first day on 21 July. On 19 August, playing for the Gentlemen of the North against the Gentlemen of the South at Meadow Road, Beeston in Nottinghamshire, he made 103, and also took four wickets for 40 runs, which was to remain his best first-class bowling analysis.

Interestingly, having played in the only first-class fixture staged at Whalley on his Lancashire debut, Hornby's appearance at Meadow Road signalled the end of first-class cricket at that venue as well.

In both 1871 and 1872 he played in both the Gentlemen versus Players matches, scoring 80 at The Oval in 1872. He was rapidly becoming one of the foremost batsmen of his generation – and his growing fame and form was to lead to an invitation to the cricketing wonderland that was North America.

Chapter Three
Voyage of discovery 1

The Monkey went in and caused much amusement by stealing runs – Robert Allan Fitzgerald

With his reputation becoming more lustrous by the match, it was in the autumn of 1872 when MCC secretary Robert Allan Fitzgerald was asked to put together an amateur side to visit North America, that Hornby was invited along with W.G.Grace. Others called on by Fitzgerald included the Hon G.R.C. (later Lord) Harris and Hornby's Lancashire team-mate Arthur Appleby.

On 8 August they left Liverpool aboard the *S.S.Sarmatian*, owned by the local Allan Line.

It was a lengthy journey and along the way meals played an important role in relieving the monotony of life on board. Breakfast was at 8 am, lunch was served at 12 noon, followed by dinner at 4 pm, tea at 7 pm and grog was available from 9 pm. As Fitzgerald, author of the seminal work, *Wickets in the West* (also known as *The Twelve in America*), wrote: 'Starvation has a bad time of it on board!'

Icebergs were seen on 15 August and during the 2,656-mile journey, which took nine days and one a half hours, whales were also spotted at sea.

In between the regular breaks for food and drink and the spotting of icebergs and marine life, there was a general air of boredom among those on board. So in an effort to avoid cabin fever, the players organised games of 'shovelboard' (sometimes called shuffleboard) and the more obscure pastime of 'ringing the pig'. Hornby devised his own boredom-beater, while the vessel lay at anchor off Greencastle, which involved jumping over as many deck chairs as he could. From one chair, the obstacle course rose eventually to five and who knows where it may have led but for the fact that Hornby, normally a surefooted hurdler, landed on his little toe and partially dislocated it, which put an end to his participation in this particular sport!

The *Sarmatian* arrived at Quebec on 17 August and, three days later, having found their land legs, the tourists took the field for their first match in Montreal. They played nine times in all, winning eight and drawing their final fixture in Boston.

After the first match there was a banquet for the 'Gentlemen of England' at which Grace made a speech, which was to be heard again and again on similar occasions during the course of the tour.

It went along the lines of 'Gentlemen I beg to thank you for the honour you have done me (sic); I never saw better bowling than I have seen today and I hope to see as good wherever I go'. The mention of bowling was interchangeable with batting as the match situation dictated and Grace sometimes used the word 'grand' instead of 'better' to describe the bowling/batting.

In Toronto on 6 September Hornby kept wicket for Fitzgerald's XII against Grace's XII to good effect with six stumpings in the two innings. They included snaring Grace, much, one would imagine, to the annoyance and irritation of the great man.

The American touring party. Back (l to r): A.Lubbock, W.G.Grace, T.C.Patteson, C.J.Ottaway. Centre: E.Lubbock, R.A.Fitzgerald, A.Appleby. Front: F.P.U.Pickering, G.R.C.Harris [who became Lord Harris a few weeks later], A.N.Hornby, W.M.Rose, C.K.Francis.

The tourists reached London, Ontario, by 10 September, where, according to Fitzgerald, 'The Monkey went in and caused much amusement by stealing runs'.

There was more amusement when the team played a two-day match against Hamilton, where the tourists arrived after a four-hour journey on the Great Western Railway, which had begun operations 19 years earlier.

By the second day the weather had deteriorated with the tourists hoping to finish the game before nightfall as they wanted to visit Niagara Falls. By 5.20 pm, the light was diminishing with the shadows growing longer by the minute. Playing against 22, the tourists, who fielded twelve men themselves, had reduced the home side to 43 for ten.

'The moon now rose,' recalled Fitzgerald, 'and an occasional cloud passing over the moon enabled the batsmen to steal runs.

'The spectators, now much amused, encroached considerably upon the wickets.

'The Englishmen now crouched upon the ground to get a sight of the ball, Hornby lying at full length, and the excitement was at its height, the last man being in, and darkness imminent. The last wicket fell to an uncompromising sneak. It was skittles rather than cricket.'

According to Alfred Gibson, reminiscing in the *Windsor Magazine* in 1897, it was so difficult to see through the murk that Hornby even lit a candle in the slips!

Fitzgerald's side finally wrapped up victory by an innings and 16 runs. But despite their efforts, it wasn't until the following day that the touring party set out to visit Niagara, where they were much taken by its 'majestic beauty and sheer grandeur'.

The St George's Club New Ground in Hoboken, New York was the next port of call, where Fitzgerald reported: 'The Monkey was in luck, and as free as his native wilds. He skied one of Greig's [deliveries] which Harry Wright carefully and deliberately dropped, to the disgust of the spectators – his 18 was very quickly if fortunately obtained.'

Only two of the home side's batsmen reached double figures in their two innings and Fitzgerald's side secured another innings victory.

On 21 September the tourists drew a crowd estimated at 7,000 to their game against Philadelphia. At the end of the match, which Fitzgerald's side won by four wickets 'the crowd collected around the clubhouse calling fondly for Grace, Ottoway, Hornby and others'.

Afterwards the local club produced an official handbook, priced at 25 cents, for what was billed as the 'International Cricket Fete at Philadelphia 1872', recalling previous matches played in 1859 and 1868.

In October 1859, George Parr's touring side had beaten the United States of America at Hoboken by an innings, while in September 1868 Edgar Willsher's XI had triumphed over the St George's Club of New York, also by an innings, on the same ground.

The 1872 handbook used quotes from William Shakespeare to describe this latest game and its players with Hornby earning this epithet: 'a snapper-up of unconsidered trifles' from Act IV, Scene II of 'The Winter's Tale'.

On their defeat, the Philadelphians reckoned this quote from the Bard fitted the bill: 'Beaten, but not without honours; [As] in this glorious and well-foughten [sic] field we kept together in our chivalry' from King Henry V, Act VI, Scene III. The Americans, in fact, added 'beaten but not without honours' to the Duke of Exeter's quote.

On 26 September the party arrived in Boston, where rain caused their game to be reduced to a single day with the team again winning as darkness fell.

Before they left Canada to set sail for home on 28 September aboard the *S.S.Prussian* there were odes of farewell written for each of the players with Hornby's reading:

> Here's to Hornby, who wears the cognomen of 'Monkey'.
> All muscle and nerve – never feeble or funky
> For pluck, skill and strength, he is hard to be beaten
> By picked men from Winchester, Harrow or Eton!

Once the tourists had climbed aboard the *S.S.Prussian* they could look back on a fascinating, eye-opening, often jaw-dropping tour of several cricketing outposts.

They had played in Ottawa, Toronto, London, Hamilton, New York and Philadelphia, feasted on roast leg of bear, visited the Niagara Falls, and much admired the American ladies 'who appeared more interested in cricket than those in England' – at least that was the view of Fitzgerald.

Finally, they arrived back at their departure point, Liverpool, on 8 October, having been away from their home comforts for two long months.

For the players the arduous tour had been a success, but cricket didn't take root to any great extent in either America or Canada as can been seen when 43 years later, in 1925, Captain T.B.Trappes-Lomax headed a mission that had been sent out to Canada to see if anything could be done about damping down the locals' sympathy for a US invasion. Trappes-Lomax reported back that Canada was 'dangerously susceptible to cultural influence from south of the border because neither cricket nor rugby had taken sufficient hold'.

Chapter Four
The Hornby-Barlow partnership begins

As the run stealers flicker to and fro, To and fro: O my Hornby and my Barlow long ago! – Francis Thompson in At Lord's

Fitzgerald's tour of North America in 1872 was an early landmark event in cricketing history and it was in that same year that Richard Gorton Barlow, known throughout his lengthy career as Dick Barlow, joined the Lancashire staff. It was to prove a pivotal moment in the club's history. Barlow opened the innings with Hornby once in the following season, but by 1875 the pair had forged the county's most illustrious first-wicket partnership. In June of that year they were presented with a bat each after they put on 148 against Yorkshire at Old Trafford, winning the match without being separated in the Lancashire second innings.

Francis Thompson aged 19, a few months after he attended the match that inspired At Lord's.

In Hornby's obituary, published on 18 December 1925 and which was probably written by Neville Cardus, the *Manchester Guardian* described Hornby and Barlow as 'a Don Quixote and Sancho Panza of the game. The one ready to tilt at windmills in high romance, the other content to go his shrewd, thrifty way and bide his time, knowing well that before the day was out he would come by his own little island of runs'.

Barlow's obituary showed just how much his alliance with Hornby improved the former's marquee value, stating:

> In the ordinary way he [Barlow] was not a batsman one would have journeyed ten miles to see, but when he opened a Lancashire innings - as he did hundreds of times - with Mr Hornby, he became a figure of extreme interest. His defence and his captain's brilliancy formed a combination fascinating to all lovers of cricket.

In fact, the pairing of Hornby and Barlow at the start of the innings became enshrined in cricketing folklore when Preston-born Francis Thompson penned his much quoted poem, *At Lord's*. Thompson wrote:

> It is little I repair to the matches of the Southron folk,
> Though my own red roses there may blow;
> It is little I repair to the matches of the Southron folk,
> Though the red roses crest the caps, I know.
> For the field is full of shades as I near a shadowy coast,
> And a ghostly batsman plays to the bowling of a ghost,
> And I look through my tears on a soundless-clapping host
> As the run stealers flicker to and fro,
> To and fro:
> O my Hornby and my Barlow long ago!
> It's Glo'ster coming North, the irresistible,
> The Shire of the Graces, long ago!
> It's Gloucestershire up North, the irresistible,
> And new-risen Lancashire the foe!
> A Shire so young that has scarce impressed its traces,
> Ah, how shall it stand before all-resistless Graces?
> O, little red rose, their bats are as maces
> To beat thee down, this summer long ago!
> This day of seventy-eight they are come up north against thee
> This day of seventy-eight long ago!
> The champion of the centuries he cometh up against thee,
> With his brethren, every one a famous foe!

The long-whiskered Doctor that laugheth the rules to scorn,
While the bowler, pitched against him, bans the day he was born;
And G F with his science makes the fairest length forlorn;
They are come from the West to work thee woe!
It is little I repair to the matches of the Southron folk,
Though my own red roses there may blow;
It is little I repair to the matches of the Southron folk,
Though the red roses crest the caps, I know.
For the field is full of shades as I near a shadowy coast,
And a ghostly batsman plays to the bowling of a ghost,
And I look through my tears on a soundless-clapping host
As the run stealers flicker to and fro,
To and fro:
O my Hornby and my Barlow long ago!

*Old Trafford in the time of Hornby and Barlow. When going out to bat,
the amateur and the professional players would have emerged from
pavilions at opposite ends of the ground, and only met in the middle.*

Thompson was a great cricket-lover and must have attended the second day of the match at Old Trafford in 1878, when the legendary W.G.Grace and his brothers, Edward (E.M.) and Fred (G.F.) were in the Gloucestershire line-up. After the visitors had taken a first innings lead of 27, Hornby and Barlow went in just before 5 pm and by close of play at 6.30 had put together a partnership of 90, with Hornby on 68 and Barlow not out 15.

The pairing of Hornby and Barlow was a classic case of opposites attracting, with Hornby in the role of Thompson's run-stealer and Barlow the obdurate, almost immoveable, object.

Showing that nostalgia is nothing new, the *Manchester Guardian* reported:

> The cricket played could not have been surpassed, even in those palmy days to which veterans still look back with real or affected regret. The 'opposition' of two such stars as Mr Hornby and Mr Grace was worth going far to see ...
>
> [Hornby] gave the spectators another proof that for skilful, hard, determined hitting, and for dexterity in stealing runs, he had only one rival on the ground ...
>
> His drives were a treat to witness, made with extraordinary force, but always keeping the ball down, and never giving the ghost of a chance ...

It's worth noting that in about 95 minutes Gloucestershire bowled 52 four-ball overs. So although the over-rate was far higher than today's, the actual rate of scoring wasn't.

Thompson's poem carries uncanny echoes of the *Manchester Guardian* article. It's hard to imagine that the writer had it to hand as he was penning his words, but perhaps he had read it and it was buried deep in his subconscious.

At Lord's is the ultimate piece of Golden Age cricket nostalgia, yet all is not as it seems. Shortly before his death and some 25 years after he had watched Hornby and Barlow bat at Old Trafford, Thompson was invited to watch Lancashire play Middlesex at Lord's. As the day of the match grew closer, he became increasingly more nostalgic. In the end Thompson did not go to the game but sat at home and wrote his poem, which had nothing to do with Lord's – neither he nor the match he describes was there!

And events on the final day could not have been further removed from our image of cricket's Golden Age. With the Grace brothers a major attraction and Hornby and Barlow going well, there was a huge crowd on hand. It grew further when working people left their factories and offices for their Saturday half-holiday. But it all turned nasty when some sections of the 18,000-strong crowd demonstrated against what they thought were inadequate arrangements for spectators. Around 2,000 had rushed the turnstiles and got into the ground for nothing and, in their anger, some of them wrenched sods of the Old Trafford turf out of the ground and hurled them around.

At the height of the melee, Hornby, who was not yet captain of the side, attempted single-handedly to restore some semblance of order. Galloping into the crowd as if pursuing a well-struck shot on its way to the boundary, Hornby grasped 'one of the most violent agitators' before handing his captive over to a policeman. According to contemporary reports, Hornby administered his own instant justice, giving the man 'a number of hard knocks' before placing him in the arms of the law.

As if the crowd trouble wasn't enough, there was also an episode reminiscent of the Sammy Jones incident in the original Ashes Test and the Ian Bell affair at Trent Bridge in the 2011 England-India series. The Lancashire amateur W.S.Patterson drove a ball to the boundary but the unsighted umpire did not signal four and a Gloucestershire player ran Patterson out. E.M.Grace went to the crowd and satisfied himself that the ball had carried, so Patterson was reinstated.

Those spectators who did pay realised gate receipts of £750, which was a tidy sum in those days. Measured against the Retail Price Index (admittedly not always the best and most reliable indicator) it would equate to a remarkable £56,000 today. What would county treasurers give for that sort of figure for three days of Championship cricket nowadays?

Unfortunately, the unruly spectators rather shot themselves in the foot when, soon after the game, Lancashire announced they were doubling the price of admission to one shilling.

In 1876, *Wisden*, reporting on Lancashire's match against Nottinghamshire at Nottingham, had this to say about the visitors' openers: 'Lancashire batting in 1876 resulted in Mr Hornby being well ahead of the others in the three important average columns, he and Barlow scoring more runs than any other seven men. Both played up to their well-known form of brilliant hitting and rapid scoring by one and stolid defence and slow scoring by the other; and perhaps their distinctively peculiar forms were never more aptly illustrated than when in Lancashire's first innings against Nottinghamshire at Nottingham the first wicket (Mr Hornby's) fell with the score as follows:

Mr A N Hornby c Selby b Oscroft..................44
Barlow not out...0
B 1
(1 wkt)   45

In fact, Barlow was at his most unyielding and carried his bat for 34 in Lancashire's all out total of 187. It was the third such instance in Lancashire's then 12-year history. Barlow was also the second Lancashire player to bat through an entire innings – against Kent at Maidstone two years earlier – and was to repeat the feat a further nine times.

Typically, he never managed to reach three figures on any of these occasions and, remarkably, against Nottinghamshire at Trent Bridge in 1882, admittedly, 'on an extremely bad wicket', he was just five not out when the tenth and final wicket went down at 69 after 87 four-ball overs. At one point he didn't score for 80 minutes. His remarkable feat of endurance earned him a place in the *Guinness Book of Records*.

So one can see why he and Hornby made such a perfect pairing.

Carrying his bat wasn't Hornby's style, but he did do so twice. He scored 23 not out in all out total of 56 in the first innings against Yorkshire at Old Trafford in June 1876. Despite Hornby's sterling effort, Lancashire lost by nine wickets. And he made 121 not out in a total of 194 all out in MCC's second innings against Cambridge University at Lord's in June 1882. He also passed 8,500 first-class runs in this match.

An extremely fit man, Hornby would frequently steal short singles and there are many tales of his running out his partner, or nearly so. Barlow said of him: 'He runs you out, then he gives you a sovereign.' W.E.Howard, the Lancashire pavilion attendant, in his entertaining book entitled *Fifty Years' Cricket Reminiscences of a Non-Player*, published in 1928, tells the story of George Yates, the Old Trafford professional. Seeking to please his captain, he ran down the wicket as the bowler delivered, only to arrive at the other end to find Hornby still in his crease and asking him: 'What the hell are you doing here, Yates?'

In 1881 Hornby was one of seven Dick Barlow victims in the Gentleman versus Players match at Lord's. Lancashire's regular opening partnership was, of course, on different sides in this fixture. Barlow's match figures were 72.2-44-55-7. Others dismissed by Barlow were W.G.Grace, Alfred Lyttelton, Bunny Lucas, Allan Steel, Arthur Trevor and Alfred Evans – 'a very tough lot, it must be admitted', said Barlow.

Hornby is commemorated by a stained-glass window which now takes pride of place in the Old Trafford Long Room. Also featured are Dick Barlow and Lancashire's splendid wicket-keeper, Richard Pilling. The window was the brainchild of Barlow, who decided to spend some of the proceeds of his benefit match in 1886 by commissioning the window, which he designed himself – he was later to design his own gravestone, which bears the inscription 'Bowled at Last'. The window was completed a year after Barlow's benefit. Pictured behind the three players is the original Old Trafford pavilion and Ladies' pavilion.

For many years the window's whereabouts were unknown until in the 1960s Lancashire historian, museum curator and committee member Keith Hayhurst, a former schoolmaster, decided to track it down. Enlisting the help of *Manchester Evening News* cricket writer and author Brian Bearshaw, the window was eventually traced. One day, Hayhurst was making inquiries about the window in Blackpool when he spotted a bowls player with a bag bearing the initials LBW. It was none other than Leslie Barlow Wilson, who was Dick Barlow's grandson. Yet neither he nor his family seemed keen to discuss the window. Barlow, it transpired had fathered an illegitimate son, who had bought the window from Barlow's daughter. It wasn't until seven years later after knocking on scores of doors that Hayhurst finally found the owner – and the window – in a house in Southport. It was taken to Old Trafford and, for some time, languished in a store room at the ground before eventually being restored to its rightful place as the centrepiece of the Long Room in the pavilion.

In addition to Francis Thompson's *At Lord's*, Hornby was celebrated in song by Dick Barlow. The first line 'Captain Hornby is the finest man for many miles around' gives some idea of the esteem in which he was held by Barlow. The latter continued his near hero-worship of Hornby by dedicating his 1908 book, *Forty Seasons of First-Class Cricket* to his former opening partner, writing: 'This book is respectfully dedicated to my old and highly-esteemed friend and colleague, A.N.Hornby, Esq, for many years Captain and President of the Lancashire County C.C.' There was also a dance by the British light music composer A.N.Norman, which celebrated the deeds of the Lancashire captain, entitled *Hornby Schottische.*

Hornby and Barlow were almost inseparable as opening partners for Lancashire – and they are still together quite close to Old Trafford in the form of Hornby Road and Barlow Road, about a three-minute walk from the ground. The two suburban roads are not quite 22 yards apart but they are no more than 100 yards

Perhaps one of the more unusual dedicatees for a piece of music.

from each other. Hornby Road, which is nearer to Old Trafford football ground than Barlow Road, contains 26 semi-detached houses. There is, appropriately, also a Hornby Drive in Nantwich.

The *Guardian*'s Marina Hyde introduced Hornby and Barlow into her column on 26 February, 2009. In a piece about the England and Wales Cricket Board employing head hunters Odgers Ray to help in their search for a new coach to replace Peter Moores, Hyde reported that Odgers Ray chief executive Simon Cummins explained that the new coach 'should have a skillset that can be respected by all stakeholders'. Hyde wrote:

> The ECB might feel unwilling to take another lesson in refinement so soon after the last one, but it would be nice to think we could keep this sort of toss out of cricket, which has always seemed so much more elegantly addressed in language we can actually understand, say, or perhaps in Francis Thompson's famous poem *At Lord's*, than by chaps who bang on about stakeholders.

'For the field is full of shades as I near a shadowy coast, and a ghostly batsman plays to the bowling of a ghost' – Yes, yes, Francis, but do tell us about your Hornby and your Barlow's skillsets.

Moores was sacked as England coach in January 2009 after a rift with the then-captain Kevin Pietersen and was appointed Lancashire coach five weeks later. In 2011, he led the Red Rose county to their first outright County Championship win in 77 years.

Caricature drawn at Old Trafford in 1887, when Hornby caught two off Barlow who took 8 for 26 in Nottinghamshire's first innings.

Chapter Five
Married to Sport

He hits at nearly every ball and is very quick on his legs. He takes guard or rather takes no guard, for his bat is fully four inches from his leg stump and thus the bowler has a full view of the wicket – Tom Horan on Hornby

Family man

They say 'money goes to money' and that is exactly what happened in 1876 when Hornby married 22-year-old Ada Sarah Ingram. She was the daughter of Herbert Ingram, the MP for Boston in Lincolnshire and founder and proprietor of *The Illustrated London News*, who had drowned in an accident on Lake Michigan sixteen years earlier. The business was later taken over by Ada's brothers William (MP for Boston at the time of her marriage) and Charles.

Illustrated London News for 18 October 1862, showing the unveiling of a memorial to its founder, Herbert Ingram, in his native Boston, Lincolnshire. Ingram was the father of Hornby's wife, Ada Sarah.

Albert and Ada were married on 17 October – the feast day of St Ethelbert – at the Parish Church, Oatlands, near Weybridge in Surrey on an unseasonably warm autumnal morning. The Reverend John Richard Armitstead officiated. He was Hornby's brother-in-law and a fellow cricketer, who played a number of games for Cheshire.

The couple set up home at Bridge House, Church Minshull, a village six miles north of Nantwich. The 1881 census records that they lived there with their four sons – aged three, two, one year and six months.

There was also a staff of five servants made up of Annie Wiley and Maria Wormleighton, both nurses, Laura Snow, a housemaid, Maria Rose, a cook and 53-year-old Thomas Halsey, a butler. It all sounds rather grand but servants, of whom some 1.4 million were employed at that time in the United Kingdom, were not expensive additions to the family's outgoings. Laura Snow would have been paid as little as £24 a year, while Thomas Halsey, the butler, might have received an annual income of around £50. Annie Wiley and Maria Wormleighton, the two servant nurses, were at the bottom of the food chain as far as wages were concerned, earning between £10 and £15 each per annum for looking after the Hornby boys.

Hornby would also have probably employed a head groom or stable master at between £30 and £50 per year and a number of stable lads, each costing between £6 and £12 per annum, to look after his string of hunters. With a large estate to oversee, Hornby would also have called on the services of a number of gardeners and odd job men.

The 1881 census records Albert's occupation as Captain 1st Royal Cheshire Militia. He received his commission in 1877 and apparently resigned in 1888.

In 1887 the family moved to an address in Nantwich, Parkfield in Wellington Road, where they lived until Ada's death in 1927. It had 16 rooms and was set in about 20 acres. According to a sketch in the 30 August 1887 edition of the *Athletic Journal*, 'cattle grazed in total ignorance of the grandeur of their surroundings' and there was also 'a farm yard, which includes a piggery, duckery and henery [sic]'.

In 1891 they had four female and two male servants, in 1901 two female and two male, and in 1911 four female.

Playing the role of the local squire to a nicety Hornby would drive around in a pony and trap, only using a carriage and pair on special occasions. Later in life when president of Lancashire he would arrive at the ground in a chauffeur-driven limousine.

The Hornbys' first born was **Albert Henry (1877-1952)**, who was educated at Harrow (as were all his brothers) and Trinity College, Cambridge. Like his father, he played for Lancashire and between 1899 and 1914 he featured in 283 matches, only nine fewer than his father. He was captain of the side from 1908 until 1914, and was embroiled in a series of disputes with the committee towards the end of the 1913 season. (See Chapter Nine.).

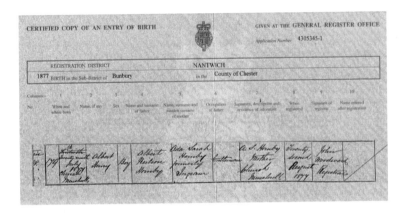

Albert Henry Hornby's birth certificate. Note that his father describes himself as a 'gentleman'.

Their second son was **Walter Ingram (1878-1918)**, who served as a private in the 32nd Australian Infantry. He died in Oxford a week before the end of the war, of wounds received in France, and was buried at home in the churchyard of St Mary's, Acton. He never married.

Hornby and Sara's third child was **George Vernon (1879-1905)**, who died in South Africa, having served in the Second South African (Boer) War. His wife and daughter settled in Nantwich. George played some cricket, including with his father, but not at first-class level.

The fourth and final offspring was **John (1880-1927)**, who in 1904 emigrated to Canada. He became a famous explorer, trapper and prospector, looking for gold and silver. In 1914 he returned to England to serve in the First World War, in which he was wounded and awarded the Military Cross. Two years later he went back to Canada and became known as the 'hermit of the north' for living with limited supplies off the 'barren lands' of the North-West Territory.

He successfully advocated the creation of a wildlife sanctuary in the area of the Thelon River, but in 1927 he and two companions died of starvation after spending a year in a cabin there. His body wasn't found until 1929, two years after his mother died. Hornby Point and Hornby Fort were named after him, and he has been the subject of several biographies and plays.

With one in Australia, one in South Africa and one in Canada, the Hornby boys obviously had itchy feet.

The year after A.N. wed, Hornby's younger brother, Charles Herbert, married Ada's sister Marguerite. The marriages helped ensure the financial security of the Hornby brothers for the foreseeable future. After 1881, when Charles was a farmer in Northamptonshire, both described themselves on censuses as 'living on own means'.

An all-round sportsman

A.N. rode to hounds from an early age and kept a stable of up to a dozen horses in Cheshire, three for his wife and the rest for himself. A fearless, and some would say, reckless rider, he drove his horses hard and in one season three were killed under him. As the *Athletic Times* told its readers on 30 August 1887: 'If you were a horse it does not sound like a good idea to join his stable.'

The article went on: 'The hunters all show signs of their master's courage as swollen knees and bandaged shins are seen in every stall.'

Vanity Fair's view in 1891 also underlined Hornby's fearless demeanour in the saddle, stating: 'He is among the best riders to hound in Cheshire, among whom he is quite the boldest.'

He was a good shot and loved blazing away at small birds and animals – and one or two gamekeepers, it was reputed! In 1887 A.N. leased the shooting rights at Dorfold Hall from his hunting friends, the Roundells. It was within easy reach of his home at Parkfield.

He was also a useful boxer and occasionally sparred with professionals. When he toured Australia in 1878 Hornby engaged

Jem Mace, the first world champion in the sport, to give him boxing lessons at a cost of £10. Norfolk-born Mace arrived in Sydney on 3 March 1877 from San Francisco. It was a year later, when Hornby was Down Under with Lord Harris's touring party and Mace was running a successful boxing academy in Melbourne, that the pair would have met in the ring.

Hornby played Rugby Union for Lancashire and at club level for Preston Grasshoppers and Manchester, then one of the strongest sides in the country. Initially he turned out for the Brookhouse Club, a team made up of workers employed in the Hornby mills. They played to the Harrow rules, a crude version of what is now association football or soccer, so at first A.N. didn't understand Rugby.

In a game against Manchester, William MacLaren, uncle of A.C. MacLaren, Hornby's successor as Lancashire cricket captain, was rushing towards Hornby who called out, 'What am I to do?' 'Tackle him,' was the reply but, not knowing exactly what a tackle was, he charged MacLaren heavily with his shoulder and knocked him backwards!

But, as in all forms of sport and, indeed, in life itself, Hornby was a quick learner and soon grasped the rules of Rugby.

Hornby learnt the rules well enough to be capped by England nine times between 1877 and 1882, making his debut against Ireland at The Oval, where he scored the only try of his international career. He played his last game for England at Whalley Range, Manchester, against Scotland. Interestingly, on the team sheet, he was listed as Monkey Hornby.

It was said that Hornby was so keen on shooting that he declined an England Rugby Union cap in 1883, preferring instead to go on a weekend shoot.

He later refereed at Rugby and was a member of the Rugby Union Committee.

At soccer he was good enough to play for Blackburn Rovers in their first match, a friendly against Partick Thistle on 2 January 1878, and in a few subsequent matches. Blackburn won 2-1 in that inaugural fixture with the home side's goals being scored by Richard Birtwistle. In one of those Rovers' appearances, in 1882, Hornby scored a goal in an FA Cup tie against Sheffield FC. He would have felt at home playing football for Rovers as their

THE ALL ENGLAND
CRICKET & FOOTBALL JOURNAL
·AND ATHLETIC REVIEW·

No. 4.—Vol. I.   JULY, 1877.   Price Twopence.

A. N. HORNBY, ESQ.

Photographed from Life by John Frankland, Preston New Road, Blackburn.

An all-round sportsman made an appropriate cover image for an all-round sports magazine.

home ground between this inaugural match and 1881 was, in fact, Alexandra Meadows.

At the time Blackburn was a hotbed of football with Rovers' local rivals including Blackburn Olympic, winners of the FA Cup at Kennington Oval in 1883 in front of an estimated 8,000 spectators. Blackburn Olympic played a significant role in the social development of the game. When they secured that FA Cup triumph they were the first team from a working-class background to do so. Previously the cup had been dominated by wealthy amateurs and Olympic's victory against Old Etonians persuaded the game's rulers, the Football Association, to allow professionalism two years later. Ironically, this decision signalled the death knell for Olympic who were unable to compete with wealthier and better supported clubs in the new professional era and were forced to fold in 1889.

But Rovers were the predominant team in the town, remarkably winning the FA Cup five times in the next eight years after Olympic's sole success in the competition. At the time of writing, Rovers have won it just once since (1928) in the intervening 120 years. They won the Premier League title in 1995 but, 17 years later, in May 2012, they were relegated to the Championship.

Just as in cricket Hornby extended his football-playing career and in 1886, eight years after that game against Partick, he was turning out for Nantwich Town against Crewe Alexandra in the semi-final of the Cheshire Cup. He was later elected president of the club, which had been founded two years earlier. They are now semi-professional, and members of the Evo-Stik Northern Premier League.

Hornby later became president of the Lancashire Football Association, and is remembered – warts and all – in this remarkably frank appraisal which forms part of the history of that organisation:

> He carried his strict methods of refereeing into all phases of his work. Only his closest friends understood him, for he was so obsessed with his own ideas, so convinced that his judgement was always right, and he had so little sympathy with anyone who did not act as he thought they ought; that he was at times a stormy petrel and never hesitated to attack, in what seemed to many of us the most savage and violent fashion, some of his best friends.
>
> At times [he was] too hasty in jumping to conclusions and too prone to regard a rumour as true, and guilt before proof had been tendered, there was a danger of him doing the very thing he prided himself that he would never do, that was to act unfairly.
>
> There were times when I almost felt that he went out of his way to interfere with matters that did not concern him, and it became necessary for someone to act as peace-maker.
>
> Occasionally he conceived some new idea and with so much faith in himself he believed in its serviceability. At times it might have been better had he exercised a greater patience before committing himself and taken counsel of others.

First tilt at the Australians

In May 1878, just four months after playing in Blackburn Rovers' first-ever match, Hornby walked out on to the field at Lord's together with W.G.Grace to open the MCC innings against the Australian tourists. The match was scheduled for three days, but with ball well on top of bat it was completed in a single day.

Grace failed in both innings, making four and nought, but Hornby top-scored in MCC's first knock with 19 out of just 33 all out. Tom Horan, writing in *Horan's Diary*, said: 'Hornby enjoyed a charmed life; he was given not out caught behind before scoring and should have been both stumped and run out.'

Horan adds: 'Hornby created a diversion for the crowd by hitting [Harry] Boyle for four through the skylight of the billiard room adjoining the club's rackets court.'

Later Horan adds:

> In his second over Spofforth levelled Hornby's leg stump for 19. This was a tremendous blow in our favour for Hornby is a very dangerous player.
> He hits at nearly every ball and is very quick on his legs. He takes guard or rather takes no guard, for his bat is fully four inches from his leg stump and thus the bowler has a full view of the wicket.
> The Lancashire star is only about 5ft 7in high, is very compactly built, and looks as if he would never tire.

Horan was certainly impressed with Hornby's batting, writing: 'Mr Hornby is a magnificent bat with upright style. He is strong in defence and back play and is a free all-round hitter. In the field he is unsurpassed and has the great advantage of being an ambidexter [sic].'

Unfortunately, in the second innings, Hornby's stamina wasn't tested. He was struck on the head by Spofforth, who was taking the first steps on the road to becoming Hornby's bête noir. Hornby retired with the score on one for four but pluckily resumed his innings, by which time MCC had slumped even further to 17 for seven, with the help of a runner only to see his partner at the other end, George Vernon, bowled by Spofforth.

Hornby himself was bowled by Boyle for one. Boyle finishing with six for three and match figures of nine for 17 although, remarkably, they were bettered by Spofforth's match analysis of ten for 20, including a hat-trick, as the Aussies strolled to a nine-wicket victory. MCC had 13 ducks in the match!

This was the second match of an arduous 39-match four-month tour for the Australians, who in addition to playing against many of the counties, also featured in games against less well-known teams including Batley, Longsight, Birmingham, Hunslet, Stockport, Hull, Crewe, Rochdale and Sunderland. It sounds more like a football or Rugby League fixture list than a cricket tour programme.

Even though Hornby was dismissed for nine (c Spofforth b Boyle) in his only innings against the Australians when appearing for the Gentlemen of England at Prince's Cricket Ground in Chelsea the following June, Horan had most definitely not changed his mind about A.N.'s prowess as a cricketer. He stuck to his guns, writing: 'I have already alluded to the Melbourne match and I still maintain the opinion expressed viz that he [Hornby] is a very hard hitter and nothing more.

'As a fielder he is unsurpassed, save by [George] Strachan and returns with right or left hand, just as the ball reaches him.'

But Horan was far from impressed with Hornby's performance in this particular encounter, writing: 'Hornby was fortunate to survive a catch and an easy stumping off two successive Boyle deliveries and was [eventually] caught by Spofforth [off the bowling of Boyle] for a wretchedly obtained nine.'

A month later Hornby was in action against the Australians again when Lancashire took on the touring team at Old Trafford. Hornby once again fell to his nemesis, Spofforth, failing to score in either innings of a drawn encounter.

Horan, as usual, had plenty to say about Hornby, writing: 'In Mr A.N.Hornby, it [Lancashire] has one of the best bats in England although he has shown miserable cricket against us so far this season. He likes a fast wicket and can't play on a sticky one. Hornby forms a formidable partnership with R.G.Barlow, stone-waller, and one of the most difficult batsmen to get out.'

Horan then turned his attention to the Lancashire ground and its supporters. He described Old Trafford thus: 'The ground is one of England's largest and finest and is kept in splendid order. In size it occupies the same area as the Melbourne ground and it possesses a good pavilion with a bar attached.'

Of the fans he wrote: 'They are very partial to the local men. When one of their own hit a fourer [sic] or did a smart piece of fielding the applause was loud and long. When one of us did likewise the silence was profound.'

But Horan might have been viewing Lancashire's HQ with red rose-coloured spectacles, for his remarks were totally at odds with a reader of the locally-based *City News* who wrote in that newspaper in 1877: 'The accommodation at Old Trafford is notoriously meagre in the extreme; the handsome pavilion will accommodate a mere handful; and as for refreshment - well, the less said the better... it must indeed be an enthusiast who will encounter a nine-hour imprisonment in the bleak and comfortless Old Trafford cricket ground.'

Plus ça change, plus c'est la même chose.

Chapter Six
Voyage of discovery 2

Hornby was struck in the face and had his shirt nearly torn off his back. He, however, conveyed his prisoner to the pavilion in triumph – Lord Harris on the Sydney riot

In October 1878 Hornby was off on his travels again – this time as part of Lord Harris's tour of Australia. Cricket was certainly giving Hornby the chance to see the world.

At about 3.15 pm on 17 October 1878, Hornby departed Southampton aboard the P & O's aptly-named *S.S.Australia* as part of Harris's team to tour Down Under. They left behind them family and friends – and a severe English winter.

Unlike previous tours – and this was the fifth to visit Australia from these shores – Harris led a group that was almost entirely comprised of amateurs. In fact, there were only two professionals among the party who were waved off from the dockside by a large crowd of well-wishers.

The two who earned their living from the game were both Yorkshiremen, George Ulyett (1851-98), who was born and died at Pitsmoor, near Sheffield, and Tom Emmett (1841-1904), who hailed from Halifax. The pair had previously visited Australia with James Lillywhite's team in 1876-77. They would do the bulk of the bowling for Lord Harris's team.

Happily, Hornby's Lancashire team mate Vernon Royle, the son of a Manchester doctor, an outstanding athlete and one of the finest cover-points of his era, kept a diary of the tour. So we know quite a bit about what happened on their visit.

It seems it was far from a smooth passage, and Royle, among others, was a poor sailor. Many of his diary entries detail just how sea-sick he was, especially in the early part of the journey from England to Gibraltar and then again on the Aden-Galle (Ceylon) leg.

Three days before arriving in Galle, Royle notes that Hornby's wife Ada was 'not at all well'. Hornby and Lord Harris were the only members of the touring party who were accompanied by their wives. Unfortunately, Hornby's reaction to his wife's condition is not recorded.

Despite the scourge of sea-sickness, the journey must have been a true voyage of discovery with Royle reporting that they saw flamingos, pelicans, porpoises, sharks and whales. One day the ship was followed by a flock of albatross.

But despite all these distractions and attractions, the tourists managed to play improvised games of cricket on board – whenever sea-sickness permitted.

On reaching Ceylon, now Sri Lanka, the tourists switched to another vessel, the *S.S.Assam* and en route to their first sight of Australia, they once again encountered heavy swells.

Royle's first glimpse of Australia came at around 7 am on Thursday 28 November when the *Assam* was 100 miles off King George Sound. They finally made land at 4.30 that afternoon.

They sailed on to Adelaide which they reached on Monday 2 December, disembarking at Glenelg, seven miles from Adelaide, at around midnight. It was here that Royle noted that they 'left Hornby and Harris with the ladies at the Crown and Sceptre'.

Having regained their land legs the touring party played their first real game on Thursday 12 December when, fielding twelve men, they took on Eighteen of South Australia at the Adelaide Oval. Nine days earlier Harris had sent a cable from the ship asking whether it would be possible to play twelve men as this was the first game of the tour.

The South Australians had no objection, not surprisingly as they themselves fielded eighteen – three more than the originally agreed fifteen. There was another pre-match problem when South Australia's Surrey-born medium-pace bowler James Goodfellow demanded the sum of one guinea per day for his services. The South Australian Cricket Association told Goodfellow they could only offer him half that figure, the amount he had previously been granted. Goodfellow refused to play and was banned for the rest of the season.

There were more problems when a planned dinner to mark the arrival of the tourists was cancelled when none of Adelaide's

Lord Harris's side in Australia, 1878/79.
Standing (l to r): F.Penn, A.J.Webbe, C.A.Absolom, S.S.Schultz [later Storey],
L.Hone (wk). Seated: F.A.MacKinnon, A.N.Hornby, Lord Harris (capt), H.C.Maul,
G.Ulyett. On the ground: A.P.Lucas, V.P.F.A.Royle, T.Emmett.
Harris and Hornby were later to fall out over Schultz's birth qualification for
Lancashire (see page 82).

leading caterers were willing to organise such a function.

Once off-field matters had been sorted out, Hornby managed 78 out of an all-out total of 185 in the tourists' first innings in reply to the home side's 110. Hornby hit just three fours in a three-hour stay, according to CricketArchive, but he did manage a five.

According to Royle, the South Australians were bowled out for 135 in their second innings, leaving the visitors to score a modest 63 for victory, but they lost seven wickets in doing so. Hornby, once again, was the top scorer, making 22.

Here, Royle seems to have got his figures in a twist, *Wisden* reckoning that SA's second innings ended on 137. On Royle's own figures Lord Harris's side would have needed 61 and not 63. Perhaps the sea-sickness had taken its toll on Royle's arithmetic!

It was estimated that the first day's attendance totalled 3,300, which grew to 9,300 over the three days with gate receipts for the match reaching a very healthy £536. The local newspaper, *The*

Register, reported on the large number of carriages at the ground 'with at least 750 ladies present in the members' enclosure'.

The social aspects of the tour seemed as important as the cricketing side and the tourists visited the theatre, the concert hall and were wined and dined on countless occasions. They also did their fair share of hunting and shooting although fishing didn't seem to be on the agenda. Together with fellow-tourist Bunny Lucas, Royle managed to ferret out 30 rabbits after their host, William Robertson, had bagged no fewer than 300 pigeons. They would have lunched well that particular day. Robertson had earlier earned his own piece of sporting fame as a member of the winning Oxford crew in the 1861 Boat Race.

On Christmas Eve, Hornby played for the tourists at Yarra Bend against Fifteen of the Melbourne Club and made 36 in a total of 434. Many of the tourists 'got out on purpose', said Royle. It seemed a rather pointless exercise as this was the only day's play. But perhaps the tourists' rather cavalier attitude might have been because the game wasn't part of the official tour programme.

The tourists' first real examination came in their timeless match against the Australians – and they failed badly. Played at Melbourne – and recognised retrospectively as a Test – the game started on 2 January. The home side needed just three days to defeat Lord Harris's XI by ten wickets.

Hornby, making his Test debut as were eight of his colleagues, had a miserable time, falling for two and four, on both occasions a victim of Spofforth, who had a remarkable match.

But Hornby did manage to take the wicket of Australia's No. 7 Frank Allan with what was described by *Wisden* as 'a grub'. In fact, he was unplayable, recording the amazing figures of 7-7-0-1. Hornby's bowling style is listed as unknown by CricketArchive and is not mentioned at all by cricinfo, but he was certainly ambidextrous (see previous reference in Chapter Four), sending down deliveries with either hand.

Spofforth's figures were even more eye-catching and he became the first bowler to achieve a Test hat-trick when he dismissed Royle, Francis MacKinnon and Emmett in the tourists' first innings as part of his six for 48 analysis. He went one better in the second innings with seven for 62. For good measure, Spofforth made his highest Test score of 39.

England never recovered from losing their first seven wickets for a meagre 26 and Australia ran out comfortable and deserved winners.

Hornby was in much better form in the game against Southern Tasmania, making 61 not out in a match the tourists won by six wickets. Played at the picturesque Lower Domain Ground in Hobart – flanked on one side by Mount Wellington and on another by the River Derwent – the game, which started on 9 January, was played in beautiful, sunny conditions.

Although Lord Harris's side won easily they might have finished off the hosts even quicker had they not had to attend a ball at Hobart Town Assembly Hall on the evening of the first day, which necessitated the day's play being cut short. There was another ball on the second evening, this time at Government House, with Royle reporting that almost all the tourists attended.

'The Disturbance'

The visitors lost to New South Wales in Sydney on 24-28 January with Hornby having a fairly undistinguished game with bat and ball. The ground was known then as Moore Park or the Association Ground and later became world famous as the Sydney Cricket Ground (SCG).

But in the second match against NSW, starting on 7 February Hornby seems to have tamed, temporarily at least, his bête noire, Spofforth. Hornby top-scored with 67 before being bowled by 'The Demon', although it didn't stop Spofforth from taking five for 93. Hornby and Bunny Lucas made the first ever century partnership in Australia, putting on 125 before Spofforth bowled Lucas for 51. It was the only time in the match that Hornby batted as the tourists' 267 proved well beyond the home side who could only muster 177 and 49, subsiding, rather tamely, to defeat by an innings and 41 runs.

Chiefly responsible for the victory was Yorkshire left-arm Emmett, who returned figures of eight for 47 and four for 13 for a match analysis of twelve for 60, one of the 29 occasions he captured ten or more wickets in a game in a career in which he finished with 1,572 first-class wickets. He began with a fast round-arm action, but as the years took their toll, he changed his style completely and ended up as a medium-pacer, using flight, spin and change of pace to great effect.

George Ulyett played his part, too, taking four in four balls as part of his analysis of four for 13 in NSW's second innings capitulation.

But the match will always be remembered for crowd trouble on the second day which soured relations between the visitors and their hosts. At the same time it underlined Hornby's bravery or foolhardiness, depending on what view one takes of his actions in the wake of the shenanigans.

As was customary in those days, Harris's side was accompanied by its own umpire, a 22-year-old Victorian called George Coulthard, a professional at Melbourne CC. He had been recommended to Harris by the club on the touring party's arrival in Australia, and had stood without incident in the match between Australia and Harris's XI that was retrospectively recognised as a Test match.

On that second day, which was a Saturday, with more than 10,000 spectators in the ground, the home side collapsed after lunch and was forced to follow on.

NSW had moved to 19 without loss in their second innings when, as *Wisden* put it with masterly understatement, there came 'The Disturbance'. It all kicked off, if you'll forgive the use of a footballing phrase, when local hero Billy Murdoch was adjudged run out by Coulthard for ten. The 19-year-old had top-scored in the first innings, carrying his bat for 82, and NSW supporters were pinning their hopes on a similar performance from Murdoch in their second knock.

It was, by the very nature of most run-out decisions, a close call, but the majority of players and spectators felt, obviously without the modern-day benefits of slow-motion playbacks, that Coulthard had just about got it right.

Coulthard, however, was already under pressure for a ruling on the first day which had been criticised by the *Sydney Morning Telegraph*. Fanning the already flickering flames was the fact that it was believed that some large bets had been struck by spectators with local bookmakers – and lost – on the Murdoch dismissal.

Before Murdoch had even reached the pavilion, a near-riot had broken out among the members.

As Harris's side waited, no batsman emerged to replace Murdoch, and Harris himself had to go to the pavilion to ask Dave Gregory, the NSW captain, what was going on. Gregory refused to send in his next batsman and insisted that the umpire be changed before the match could continue. Harris stood firm and refused. The tourists 'considered the [run out] decision a good one', according to Royle.

It was rumoured that Gregory's stance had been encouraged by gamblers. Royle, writing in his diary, felt that Gregory had been persuaded by some of the 'better class in the pavilion'. Royle himself makes no mention of gambling having anything to do with the affair, feeling it was all down to the 'larrikins' as he calls them. A 'larrikin', incidentally, is Australian or New Zealand slang for what is euphemistically described as 'a mischievous person'.

There is no doubt that Australia between 1870 and 1900 was, in parts, a lawless society. Gangs roamed the streets at night and in the early hours of Sunday morning, a few hours after the Sydney riot, about 400 miles away in the small town of Jerilderie, the infamous Ned Kelly and his cohorts robbed the bank. The gang got away with more than £2,000 after imprisoning the town's two policemen in their own cell, dressing in their uniforms before strolling down the main street informing the locals they were reinforcements from Sydney. Kelly was convicted of killing three policemen in an incident earlier in the same year when he was hiding out in the bush. In 1880 he was hanged at Old Melbourne Gaol, now a major tourist attraction with the Ned Kelly story its main feature.

Meanwhile, back in Sydney, as the two captains talked, some of the angrier spectators started climbing over the low fencing that surrounded the playing area and headed menacingly towards the middle. Harris tried to protect Coulthard, the target of the mob, and was himself struck by a stick although he wasn't badly hurt.

Hornby, displaying more recklessness than fear, armed himself with a stump and waded into the mob, grabbing Coulthard's assailant before frog-marching him to the pavilion, fighting off blows all the way and having his shirt almost ripped from his back for his troubles. He handed over the man to a member of the local constabulary.

'He [Hornby] was struck in the face,' wrote Harris later, 'and had his shirt nearly torn off his back. He, however, conveyed his prisoner to the pavilion in triumph.' Later, the Sydney Cricket Association downgraded Hornby's bravery somewhat, describing the Lancastrian's prisoner as 'a supposed offender of very diminutive stature'. It was also reported that Hornby had grabbed the wrong man!

Emmett and Ulyett picked up stumps for self defence, but the tourists remained on the field. 'For some thirty minutes or so I was surrounded by a howling mob,' Harris explained, 'resisting the entreaties of partisans and friends to return to the pavilion until the field was cleared, on the grounds that if our side left the field the other XI could claim the match.'

The outfield was eventually cleared, but Harris and Gregory remained at odds, until finally Gregory stomped off announcing the game was at an end. Harris asked Edmund Barton, the other umpire, to speak to Gregory, successfully persuading him to change his mind about keeping the NSW side off the field. Twenty-three years later Barton was elected Australia's first prime minister, and it was believed that the publicity he received for his peace-keeping efforts helped him take the first step towards that role, when he won a state lower house seat later in 1879.

Meanwhile, the crowd had once more stormed onto the field which again had to be cleared.

Finally, Alick Bannerman and Nat Thomson came out to resume the NSW innings, but before the first ball could be bowled, the crowd invaded for a third time. This time they couldn't be shifted and play was eventually abandoned for the day. Harris and his players refused to leave the playing area until the official close of play. 'Beyond slyly kicking me once or twice the mob behaved very well!' observed the skipper.

After a pause for reflection on the Sabbath, the game resumed on Monday without any further interruptions. By now rain had affected the pitch and Harris's XI wrapped up an innings victory as the NSW innings subsided quickly.

Initially, the local press condemned the riot, with the *Sydney Morning Herald* calling it 'a blot upon the colony for some years to come', while the *South Australian Register* said it was 'a disgrace to the people'.

But the *SMH* also pointed out that 'one of the English professionals made use of a grossly insulting remark to the crowd about their being nothing but sons of convicts and this no doubt had something to do with their frenzied excitement which arose all at once, and incited the crowd to acts of violence'.

The matter, though, was far from over, and the publication of a letter from Harris about the incident stirred up a veritable hornet's nest.

Harris's letter was published in London on April 1 and it changed the mood discernibly. In an extremely lengthy epistle Harris began: 'I am not certain whether you will be astonished or not at what I have to tell you, but I know you will be distressed that your friends, a party of gentlemen travelling through these Colonies for the purpose of playing a few friendly games of cricket, should have been insulted and subjected to indignities it distresses us to look back upon.'

Harris, clearly warming to his task, described what had happened to Hornby after he (Harris) had been 'struck by some larrikin with a stick'.

Harris went on: 'Hornby immediately seized this fellow and in taking him to the pavilion was struck in the face by a would-be deliverer of the larrikin and had his shirt nearly torn off his back. He, however, conveyed his prisoner to the pavilion in triumph.'

Later Harris accused the NSW members of being instrumental in the disturbances. He wrote: 'The disgraceful part of the business is that other members of the association – one a member of the legislative assembly – aided and abetted the bookmakers in raising the cry.'

The NSW Cricket Association (NSWCA) replied in kind, but at not such length, their honorary secretary J.M.Gibson, expressing regret but accusing Harris of being economical with the truth, claiming that Lord Harris had earlier told a deputation from the NSWCA that he did not hold the association in any way responsible for what had happened.

The association also claimed that betting was 'strictly prohibited by the trustees of the ground', although they added rather pointedly, 'so far as it can be prohibited'. The NSWCA added: 'Large placards [banning betting] have always been kept posted throughout the pavilion and its inclosures [sic]'.

In closing, Gibson, clearly riled by the accusation that those betting on the match were members of his association, added: 'The betting men to whom Lord Harris alludes, and of whom only one or two were present, were not members of this association at all, and it is completely unjust to assign the demonstration to any such agency. Bad as it was, it sprang from no mercenary motive.'

Two men, presumably 'larrikins', were subsequently charged with disorder, and several members, including a well-known bookmaker, were booted out of the NSWCA and banned from the ground. Harris cancelled the return match at Sydney, which would have been only the fourth Test ever.

In 1880, Murdoch led an Australia side to England, but such was the hostility among the cricketing hierarchy that they struggled to get any meaningful fixtures. Harris wrote: 'They asked no-one's goodwill in the matter, and it was felt this was a discourteous way of bursting in on our arrangements; and the result was they played scarcely any counties and were not generally recognised. We felt we had to make a protest against too frequent visits.'

It was only at the end of that summer that Harris was approached by Surrey to raise an England side for a Test. He agreed, although three of his selections who had been at Sydney – Hornby, Emmett and Ulyett – refused to play. It was, nevertheless, to be the first Test played in England. Prior to the Test, Australia did meet some of the counties, including Yorkshire (three times) and Gloucestershire (twice) but for most of the time they had to make do with taking on teams of the calibre of Crewe, Bradford, Burnley and District, Malton, Sunderland and Stockport. It certainly seemed like payback time even though Lord Harris tried to heal the rift between the two great cricketing powers when he spoke at a farewell dinner given in honour of the tourists at London's Mansion House.

George Coulthard was almost certainly the youngest umpire to stand in a Test match. He retired from umpiring just three years later and played some first-class cricket, including for Victoria against New South Wales. He appeared in the sixth-ever Test, Australia against England at the Sydney Cricket Ground in February 1882, batting at No.11 (six not out in his only innings) and he didn't bowl. Murdoch captained Australia in that match and some believed that Coulthard's lack of involvement in what was his only Test appearance was down to Murdoch still smarting from the run-out decision. It was Coulthard's last game as a player although he did umpire the eighth Test match on record between Australia and England at Melbourne in March 1882. He was also a top-class Australian Rules player with the Carlton club in Victoria. Three times – in 1876, 1877 and 1879 – he was the club's leading goal kicker. Tragically, he died from tuberculosis in October 1883 at the age of 27. He was inducted into the Australian Football League Hall of Fame in 1996.

The conclusion of the tour

Harris's team seemed undaunted by what had happened at Sydney and the day after the match ended, Hornby and some of the other players celebrated their victory by 'sailing all over the harbour' in a yacht that had been loaned to them for the afternoon.

Harris and his side then moved on to Victoria where they played at the Melbourne Cricket Ground (MCG). The hosts lost £6,000 staging that event – a considerable sum in those days although far less than Glamorgan and Yorkshire lost in putting on Test matches in recent years. Glamorgan suffered a £1.2m financial setback – 70 per cent of their annual operating deficit of £1.7m – when hosting the England-Sri Lanka Test in May 2011, while Yorkshire suffered losses in the region of £1m when staging the Pakistan-Australia Test in the previous year. The loss at Melbourne in 1879 wasn't due to lack of public interest as was the case at the Swalec Stadium and at Headingley Carnegie; it was put down to the monumental bar bill racked up by the England players. Maybe it was some kind of retribution for the way they had been treated in Sydney.

Hornby's next major on-field contribution came in the game against Twenty Two of Bendigo, which began on 26 February. He scored 77 not out on the first day in an unbroken first-wicket partnership with Francis MacKinnon which had reached 138 at the close. In the evening the group went to Leon's Circus 'where one of the clowns imitated Hornby's batting', although Royle doesn't explain this further!

Undaunted, Hornby went on to complete his century next morning, finally falling for 104. But the Lancastrian's effort was in vain with the match ending in a tense draw. At the close, Bendigo needed three more runs, while Lord Harris's team were still striving for the home side's twenty-first and final wicket.

Hornby made a decent score in the first innings – 86 – in the next game, against Twenty Two of Ballarat at the Eastern Oval, but wasn't required to don the pads again as Ballarat subsided by 'an innings and 40-odd runs', according to Royle's diary. CricketArchive is, as you would expect, more accurate, giving the winning margin as an innings and 48 runs.

There was just one more match remaining on what had been an exhausting three-month tour, the game against Victoria at the MCG, where Hornby scored two runs in each innings and took the same number of wickets (at a cost of nine runs) in a six-wicket win.

Hornby's bowling was miserly in the extreme and he sent down eleven maidens in his fifteen overs. Contemporaneous reports describe Hornby's deliveries as 'Sydney Grubbers'. This was a ball that was 'a fast underhand delivery aimed directly at the middle stump and at no time did ever leave the ground'.

'The MCG spectators became angry. First they chanted "why don't you have a go?" and when the difficulty of scoring off Hornby became apparent they switched to "take him off".'

Unsurprisingly, his economy rate during his entire 29-year career was a respectable 1.74 per four-ball over, but he bowled only 593 balls in first-class cricket and took just eleven wickets. In fact, Hornby was one of only 130 cricketers who are known to have bowled underarm in a first-class game, according to Gerald Brodribb's *The Lost Art – a History of Under-arm Bowling*, published in 1997.

Perhaps the most famous (or infamous) incident of underarm bowling came at the MCG a century later, when in February 1981 Australia captain Greg Chappell asked his younger brother Trevor to bowl underarm in a One-Day International against New Zealand. The Black Caps needed six runs to win off the last ball, but Trevor Chappell bowled it all along the ground, resulting in an Australia win. Afterwards, the then Prime Minister of New Zealand, Robert Muldoon, described it as 'the most disgusting incident I can recall in the history of cricket', going on to say that 'it was an act of true cowardice and I consider it appropriate that the Australian team were wearing yellow'. Even the Australian Prime Minister, Malcolm Fraser, called the act 'contrary to the traditions of the game'. On air for Australia's Channel 9 at the time, veteran commentator Richie Benaud described the act as 'disgraceful'. 'It was one of the worst things I have ever seen done on a cricket field'.

The New Zealand leg of Hornby's tour featured a one-day single innings match against a Canterbury XI, in which Lord Harris's XI was a mixed team containing five Canterbury players. Hornby opened the batting and the bowling. He scored 66 and finished with four for 53 (although the scorecard differs from his analysis, crediting him with only three wickets) in a 56-run win for the visitors.

The tourists had a long rest from cricket and weren't in action again for about six weeks, when they reached New York on 5 May. At the St George's Club in Hoboken, Lord Harris's XI played a team that called itself the United States of America, made up of club cricketers from New York and Philadelphia. Only seven of the tourists played and Harris wasn't among them, so Hornby captained the side. The numbers were made up by four local English-born players including George Lane, a Nottinghamshire man who was working as the professional at Staten Island C.C. In the home side's second innings Hornby took two wickets, bowling unchanged with Lane. The Englishmen won by an innings and 114 runs.

Two days later the tired tourists were on board the White Star Line's *S.S.Baltic* for the long journey home.

*****

Fred 'The Demon' Spofforth appeared to have the Indian sign over Hornby. But he might not have become the scourge of England's batsmen for ten years from 1877 to 1887 but for his first sight, as a ten-year-old boy, of England's fearsome fast bowler George Tarrant on his tour Down Under in 1863/4. Ten years later he saw the slow bowling of James Southerton and the medium pace of Alfred Shaw when they were touring with W.G.Grace, and resolved to combine the styles of all three men. He was unleashed

Fred Spofforth was arguably Australia's finest pace bowler of the nineteenth century, and usually proved too good for Hornby.

in his first Test against England at Melbourne in 1877, taking four wickets. He ended his career with 94 Test wickets at 18.41 and a total of 853 in first-class cricket at 14.95.

Spofforth took Hornby's wicket on no fewer than 12 occasions, bowling him ten times, having him leg before once and caught once. Obviously, Hornby was unable to fathom Spofforth's pace and movement. Spofforth's percentage of players bowled in his long and distinguished career was 53 per cent, while against Hornby it had grown to 83 per cent. Hornby's own overall record was 34 per cent bowled in his 1,010 innings.

In one match Hornby and Spofforth were team-mates, when on 19 June 1878 they and E.M.Grace turned out for C.I.Thornton's XI against Maldon. Now perhaps better known as the home club of England captain and Essex batsman Alastair Cook, Maldon was then a strong club side that five years earlier had beaten an All-England Eleven. Maldon engaged two professionals, the temperamental wicket-keeper Edward Pooley and the wily slow round-arm bowler John Hughes, who was two weeks short of his 53rd birthday. Pooley and Hughes combined to have Hornby stumped for a duck, but Maldon could not repeat their success against All-England, and lost by an innings and 30 runs.

In Maldon's second innings Hornby took five for 12, including the collector's item of 'W.Sewell c. Spofforth b. Hornby 1'. The Demon with 27 and The Boss with 43 then entertained the crowd in an exhibition second innings after the match had finished. It gives one plenty of food for thought about any conversations between the two during the course of the game.

Chapter Seven
The Boss

Having full confidence of his own opinions, Mr Hornby was the finest skipper I have seen - W.E.Howard

There is no doubt that Hornby was one of the great captains in Lancashire's history, but what is in question is exactly how many seasons he led the side. Some sources say Hornby was in charge for the period 1869-1899, but that isn't the case. After painstaking research, using CricketArchive and *Scores and Biographies*, it is probable that he led the side – either as sole captain or in a shared or stand-in role – for 19 of the 33 years he played for the county.

Edmund Rowley, who was present at the meeting at the Queen's Hotel in Manchester on 12 January 1864 when the Lancashire county club was formed, was the official captain between 1866 and 1879. But throughout the 1870s Hornby was called upon to lead Lancashire in Rowley's absence. He captained in 23 of the 26 games he played between 1876 and 1878, and no captain is recorded for one of the other three games. It was therefore no surprise that when Rowley retired at the end of 1879, Hornby was appointed captain. As Eric Midwinter put it in his book *Red Roses Crest the Caps*: 'If Edmund Rowley was the Joseph of Lancashire cricket, dreaming dreams of possible deliverance and glory, Albert Hornby was its Moses.' Hornby was certainly the official club captain between 1880 and 1891 and again in 1897 and 1898, which adds up to 14 years. He was also joint-captain with Sydney Crosfield in 1892 and 1893.

By 1881 the number of first-class matches played by the county had risen to fourteen and in this year Hornby became the first Lancashire batsman in its then 17-year history to score 1,000 runs in a season (at an average of 50.10), beating the four-figure mark by just two runs.

Hornby's reputation was growing. As a letter writer to the *Manchester Guardian* stated:

> For a number of years he has played in nearly all matches. He has always played well.

Hornby continued as Lancashire president until 1916 and regularly attended matches almost until his death. His portrait was an iconic image in the Long Room at Old Trafford.

His presence is a guarantee for a fair attendance for there are hundreds in Lancashire who will go a day's journey to see him get 50; and more than this, he has made Lancashire cricket popular with cricketers so that now our best players are proud to be asked to play for the county.

There is no doubt that Hornby welded the Lancashire side into an effective unit and that they were now a match for anyone. Before 1890 there was no agreed method of deciding the County Champions, but Lancashire, with ten wins and no defeats, were certainly the outstanding team of 1881. In 1879 and 1882 they shared the honours with Nottinghamshire, and throughout the 1880s they remained one of the stronger sides. He therefore inherited a successful team and built on that success.

W.E.Howard, in his book, recalls:

Having full confidence of his own opinions, which, to my mind, is one of the best qualifications of a good captain, Mr Hornby was the finest skipper I have seen. On the field he was a model to young players; possessed of an iron constitution and of fine physical powers, he was able to accomplish a large amount of strenuous work. I never heard him say that he was tired after a long day in the field, but, unfortunately, he did not seem to think others might be.

He told S.M.Crosfield, after the latter had said that he was tired at the close of play, that he would put him long-field at both ends next day, and he meant it.

Off the field, Hornby played an important role in Lancashire's purchase of Old Trafford. When the possibility of buying the ground came up, the honorary treasurer, James MacLaren, supported the proposal but the secretary, Sam Swire, opposed the move. Hornby threw his weight behind the plan and the committee approved it.

In 1882 Lancashire and Nottinghamshire lost one game each, so by the convention of the day were deemed joint champions. Lancashire won ten of their 14 games so perhaps had the edge over Nottinghamshire, who won eight out of 12. Standing: J.Rowbotham (umpire), G.Nash, R.Pilling, R.G.Barlow, A.Watson, J.MacLaren (Hon. Treasurer). Seated (back): J.Crossland, C.H.Haigh, A.N.Hornby, F.Taylor. Seated (front): W.Robinson, V.P.F.A.Royle, J.Briggs. Lancashire fielded the same team in four consecutive away games and former Yorkshire skipper Joseph Rowbotham umpired in all four, so was one of the few Yorkshiremen to appear in a Lancashire team photo.

James MacLaren was ambitious for the cricketing future of his seven sons and consulted Hornby, who advised him to send them to his old school, Harrow. MacLaren's money soon ran out but not before the second boy, Archie, had benefited from the coaching at Harrow. Archie was to become an even finer batsman than Hornby.

MacLaren was Harrow's star player and made his Lancashire debut at Hove on 14 August, 1890. Hornby asked him where he usually fielded and the young man, rather full of himself, replied 'Oh, anywhere except point,' – where, of course, Hornby put him for the rest of the innings. Despite, or perhaps because of, that incident, MacLaren had great respect for Hornby and in some ways modelled himself on him.

In 1890 and 1891 Hornby led Lancashire to second place behind Surrey, after which he was appointed joint captain with Sydney Crosfield. In 1894 Archie MacLaren took over as skipper and Hornby became president of the club. It had been a successful and far from uneventful fourteen years.

Lancashire had been runners-up five times in seven years, and in 1897 they at last won the Championship. They were indisputably the leading county for the first time since 1881. MacLaren stood down temporarily in 1897 and 1898, and so, appropriately, the 50-year-old Hornby led the Red Rose triumph.

His way of captaining a side did not always meet with the approval of some of the players, and those running the family business in Blackburn were said to have been relieved that he did not remain there. He had no head for business. and it is certainly true that his natural management style was outdated in industry, even in the 1870s. Like a number of young men from well-to-do families he found a place on the sporting field in which he could use his ability and expend his energy without causing any damage to the family business. On balance it was to Lancashire's advantage, and was also of benefit to both codes of football.

A great competitor

Boundary lines were brought in as a result of Hornby's energetic fielding. W.G.Grace recalls in his *Cricketing Reminiscences and Personal Recollections*, 1899:

> There were no fixed boundaries at Lord's when I first played there.
> If a ball struck the pavilion railings a four was allowed –

although even that [rule] was suspended one year – but every other hit had to be run and occasionally a ball would be hit among the spectators, who would open to let it pass through them, but often close again immediately.

Fieldsmen frequently found it difficult to get through the crowd to the ball.

On one occasion Mr A.N.Hornby was out in the long-field at Lord's when a ball was driven among the spectators.

As everybody knows, the Lancashire amateur was a very energetic fieldsman and as he dashed after the ball he scattered the crowd in all directions.

One poor old gentleman, not being sufficiently alert to get out of the way, was thrown on his back and rather severely hurt... as a result a boundary line was instituted.

Hornby was never afraid to take on board new ideas and was almost certainly the first captain in this country to dispense with the services of a long-stop. It happened in the North versus South fixture at Lord's in 1878 when Hornby, who was captaining the North, asked the Yorkshire wicket-keeper George Pinder (also known as George Pinder Hattersley) if he could keep without a long-stop. Pinder agreed and, in the event, conceded only four byes. In his book, *The History of Yorkshire Cricket*, published by Christopher Helm in 1989, former ACS member Anthony Woodhouse claims that Pinder was the first wicket-keeper to stand up to fast bowling.

A.A.Thomson, in *Cricket my Happiness*, writes:

To Pinder it was a sore point that the great Australian prince of wicket-keepers [Blackham] should regularly be credited with the honour of being the first wicket-keeper to function without a long-stop.

'I was the man,' said Pinder. The game was a North v South match, and A.N.Hornby, who was captain, asked him if he could keep wicket without a long-stop.

'Well, you know sir', said Pinder, 'every time it passes me it'll be four.'

Hornby seemed willing to take the risk and when one flyaway ball, probably from Tom Emmett, did go to the boundary, he was not alarmed. The experiment was regarded as successful.

However, the Australians will argue that their keeper, Jack Blackham, was the first to operate without a long-stop when playing for the touring team in the same year. Blackham used to become really angry when his captain insisted on a long-stop being employed. Blackham claimed, in an article in *The Referee* published in 1915, that he was definitely the first to keep without the safety net of a long stop, saying he did so when playing for East Melbourne before the 1878 tour. He was convinced that the English copied what was an Australian innovation. Whoever was first to ban the long-stop, Hornby or the Australian tourists of 1878, the fielding position hasn't been seen much since apart from in schools and junior cricket.

Hornby was an austere captain, but that is not to say he didn't have a sense of humour. As *Wisden* reported: 'A characteristic tale of the famous batsman concerned the Gentlemen and Players match at The Oval in 1881, Hornby and W.G.Grace had given the amateurs a capital start when, from a powerful drive, Hornby was magnificently caught high up in the long field by William Gunn, who stood some 6ft 3in in height. 'Bad luck, Monkey,' said a friend as Hornby passed into the pavilion. 'Yes,' answered Hornby, 'no one but a damned giraffe would have got near it.'

This 1888 photo was taken at Canterbury in front of the famous old lime tree, which was blown down in 2005. Standing: G.R.Baker, F.H.Sugg, F.Taylor, R.G.Barlow, E.E.Steel, G.Yates. Seated: S.M.Crosfield, A.N.Hornby, R.Pilling, J.Eccles. On ground: A.Watson, J.Briggs.

There are few - if any - captains who can claim to have led sides who have bowled out Australia twice in the same match for fewer than 50. Hornby achieved this distinction when skippering the North against Australia at Old Trafford in 1886 when the visitors were bowled out for 45 in their first innings and 43 in the second.

The North fared even worse in their only completed innings, being dismissed for 34. Unfortunately, rain washed out the last of the scheduled three days and the match ended in a draw with the North on 15 for one, needing 40 more to win.

Surrey were on the wrong end of a Hornby outburst in 1888 when Lancashire travelled to The Oval in August for their penultimate game of the season. Prior to the start one of the Surrey officials took Hornby into the pavilion to show off a plate that would commemorate the side's unbeaten run. Unsurprisingly, Hornby was furious and immediately after the visitors had secured a nine-wicket win, thanks in the main to a brilliant 184 from Joseph Eccles, he stormed into the committee room and smashed the plate on the table, saying, 'What do you think of your blasted plate now?'

A bowlers' captain

Bowlers must have relished playing under Hornby as he was captaining Lancashire when George Nash took four in four balls against Somerset at Old Trafford in June 1882 and again when Arthur Mold performed a similar feat against Nottinghamshire at Trent Bridge in June 1895.

He was also leading the side when Alexander Watson took three-in-three against Kent at Castleton Cricket Club Ground, Rochdale in June 1876 and when John Crossland did the same in the match against Surrey at The Oval in August 1881. Hornby was also skippering Lancashire against Derbyshire at Derby in June 1881 when Dick Barlow completed a hat-trick, and when he repeated the trick in August 1886 against Nottinghamshire at Old Trafford.

Hornby was also playing, although Edmund Rowley captained the side, when Barlow achieved the first hat-trick of his career against Derbyshire at Old Trafford in June 1879. Hornby was in Lord Harris's XI when George Ulyett took four in four balls against New South Wales at Sydney in February 1879. How many captains have had two four-in-four balls and four hat-tricks under their leadership and played in two games where a team-mate took a hat-trick and another four in four?

Hornby also featured in the Lancashire match against Hampshire at Old Trafford in July 1870 in which William Hickton returned figures of ten for 46, which remain the best in the county's history, and was captaining the side when Arthur Appleby took nine for 25 against Sussex at Hove in August 1877.

Hornby with wicket-keeper Dick Pilling (left) and two of the bowlers who took hat-tricks under his captaincy, Alec Watson (second left) and Dick Barlow (right).

It has been said that Hornby's loyalty to his professionals at this time was admirable. But some believed that his 'loyalty' was in reality often a fit of pique and a determination to get his own way, right or wrong. It was never more obvious than in his support for three of his professionals over the controversial issue of throwing.

Chapter Eight

The Crossland and Mold throwing controversies

That in playing Lancashire, the Lancashire men shall not be allowed to use bats, but only broom handles – Christmas card sent by Lancashire to Nottinghamshire

Loyalty to his players was paramount as far as Hornby was concerned and nowhere was it more clearly defined than in the controversies that engulfed fast bowler John Crossland and slow left-armer George Nash, and later another fast bowler, Arthur Mold.

John Crossland and George Nash

Crossland was only a peripheral figure in the Lancashire side during the 1881 season, playing just seven games and taking only thirteen wickets, ten of them in one game. Nash, meanwhile, had played his first game for Lancashire two years earlier and went on to take 200 wickets for the county.

It was not until 1882 that Crossland's action was called into question and there was a concerted campaign to have him banned from the game.

But it was four, often acrimonious, years before Crossland was finally chucked out of cricket. Ironically, it wasn't for throwing, it was because he was said to have failed to meet the requirements of residential qualification which was a prerequisite in that era.

In that 1882 season, Crossland became, on the retirement of William McIntyre, Lancashire's main strike bowler and towards the end of that campaign there began the first murmurings about his action.

It happened in the game against Surrey at The Oval, which Crossland went into in fine form. He had taken seven wickets in the match against the Australians and Spofforth himself had gone on record as saying that Crossland was quicker than he was.

Crossland had taken six for seven against Somerset on a very difficult Manchester wicket and took eight Kent wickets a few days later, four of his last six wickets coming in the second innings without a run being scored off his bowling.

One of Crossland's victims was Kent skipper Lord Harris, who had been Hornby's captain on the 1878/79 tour to Australia. That relationship between Hornby and Harris made little difference and the good lord was to orchestrate the attacks on Crossland's action.

Umpire Bob Thoms. In a famous exchange about throwing, Lord Harris snapped: 'When are you umpires going to do something about this?' Thoms, who had controversially given Australia's Sammy Jones run out in the Oval Test the previous year, replied: 'My Lord, we are going to do nothing. It is you gentlemen who have got to do it.'

It was a fact that Crossland was never no-balled in his entire career by a first-class umpire – a point vigorously made by Hornby, who was not shy in coming to his star bowler's defence.

The right-armer was born in the village of Sutton-in-Ashfield, Nottinghamshire, often dubbed 'the nursery of cricket' and which was the birthplace of so many famous cricketers including Johnny Briggs, Fred Morley, James Shaw and, more recently, Tim Robinson.

At times Crossland was almost unplayable and looked a certainty to be selected to play for England against Australia. In the end, he wasn't chosen, and it was rumoured that the Australians would have objected to his selection had his name been put forward.

At the start of the 1883 season, Lord Harris was again vociferous in his condemnation of bowlers – without mentioning anyone by name – who were breaking Law 10 which states that 'the ball must be bowled. If thrown or jerked, the umpire shall call "no-ball"'. Harris claimed this rule was being flouted time and again.

The 1883 season saw the introduction of 'neutral' umpires, and when Crossland and Nash bowled in the opening match of the season against Derbyshire at Old Trafford there was a collective intake of breath among the spectators until their first, crucial overs had been completed.

Surprisingly, Crossland wasn't called on by Hornby until Derbyshire followed on, taking four for 21. Nash, whose action was also coming under closer scrutiny and who was also a target of Lord Harris in his attempts to rid the game of bowlers he considered to be throwers, opened the bowling in Derbyshire's first innings. He ended with figures of five for 24 and added three for 47, again opening the bowling, in the second innings as Lancashire completed an easy innings victory. In the end, both men bowled without incident.

However, confrontation was not far away and it duly arrived – along with Kent and Lord Harris – when Lancashire hosted their southern rivals. But no exception was taken to Crossland's bowling – he took six of the last seven wickets as Kent crashed from 280 for 3 to 309 all out, Lord Harris scoring 118. In the end Lancashire scored a famous victory with Hornby man of the match with innings of 88 and 96.

But there was a further test ahead for Crossland and Nash when MCC hosted Lancashire at Lord's. It appeared that Lancashire's 'terrible twins' Crossland and Nash had modified their actions for this game and neither was called into question by the umpires.

It looked as though the controversy had died down when the return game against Kent was played at Gravesend in late August. Crossland was virtually unplayable in the Kent second innings, taking four wickets in 26 balls and including Lord Harris among his victims.

But a few days later, the return with Surrey at The Oval brought another flashpoint – and once again Hornby backed Crossland to

The Lancashire team that played Oxford University in 1883.
Standing: A.Watson, J.Crossland, R.Pilling, W.Robinson, G.Nash,
Seated: H.B.Steel, A.N.Hornby, S.M.Crosfield, E.Roper.
On ground: R.G.Barlow, J.Briggs, C.Coward (umpire). The bowling actions
of Crossland and Nash later provoked a series of confrontations
in which Hornby vigorously supported his bowlers.

the hilt. He even threatened to walk away from the game after Crossland had been shouted at and jostled by spectators as he came off the field at the close of Surrey's first innings on the first day. It was half an hour before Hornby could be persuaded to send out his openers, but he was not one of them. He asked Frank Taylor to open with Barlow and the captain was so furious he threatened never to play again with Lancashire at the ground, although later he relented and appeared there several more times before the end of his career.

The dispute rumbled on through the winter when Nottinghamshire announced their refusal to play Lancashire in the upcoming 1884 season. Nottinghamshire didn't mince words when they stated: 'Lancashire have during the last season played in their Eleven at least two men as to the fairness of whose bowling there is grave doubt.'

In December 1883 the county secretaries met to discuss the question of unfair bowling and tried to get a gentlemen's agreement, couched in rather catch-all terms 'not to employ any bowler whose action is at all doubtful'. Yorkshire, Kent, Middlesex, Derbyshire, Nottinghamshire and Surrey signed. It is believed that

Cambridge University also declined a fixture against Lancashire, but, as you would have expected in the circumstances, Lancashire and Hornby refused to be a party to any such document.

To add a little Christmas spice to the affair, Lancashire sent a Christmas card to Trent Bridge which stated sarcastically:

Cricketing Rules drawn up by Nottinghamshire CCC, 1883-84

Rule 1   That in playing Lancashire, the Lancashire men shall not be allowed to use bats, but only broom handles.

Rule 2 That Lancashire shall not be allowed any bowlers, and if so, no stumps to be used; and the Nottinghamshire captain to select the bowler.

Rule 3 That both umpires shall be strictly Nottinghamshire men.

Rule 4 That in case there is any fear that Nottinghamshire should lose, even under these rules, the Nottinghamshire men leave the field and refuse to finish the game.

Nottinghamshire weren't slow with their riposte, which took the form of a New Year's card to Old Trafford, which read:

Lancashire County Cricket Club

The only rules necessary for players in the County Eleven are that they shall neither have been born in, nor reside, in Lancashire.

Sutton-in-Ashfield men (Briggs and Crossland) will have the preference.

Crossland was once again in action against Lord Harris when Kent came calling to Old Trafford with the Kent captain showing much bravery, scoring 53 in Kent's comprehensive win despite being struck about the body by a number of Crossland deliveries.

But the issue was far from dead in the water and when the Lancashire committee chose the team for the England versus Australia Test at Old Trafford Crossland was included in the twelve along with Lord Harris. Hornby was named as captain. At this point a letter from Lord Harris was read, which once again made his feelings clear about the legitimacy of Crossland's action.

Sam Swire, the Lancashire secretary, was instructed to send the following reply: 'Dear Lord Harris, My committee have decided to play Crossland against the Australians, therefore we suppose under the circumstances the English team will lose your valuable assistance which we very much regret.'

In the end neither Lord Harris nor Crossland played and perhaps Hornby, usually more confrontational than conciliatory, was being diplomatic for once in his career.

Crossland was barracked in the remaining games he played and police reinforcements were brought in at The Oval although in the end Crossland didn't play because of an arm injury.

But Lancashire in general and Hornby in particular continued to support their player.

The fixture list saw to it that Crossland and Lord Harris would cross swords again in the opening match of the 1885 season at Old Trafford and despite his very public pronouncements Lord Harris was given a great ovation when he walked out to bat on the first day. Crossland was the bowler and his lordship played his first two balls with ease. The third delivery, however, spread-eagled his stumps and, unsurprisingly, the home crowd couldn't conceal its pleasure. The *Manchester Guardian* reported: 'People seemed fairly beside themselves with delight. Hats and coats were thrown up and one enthusiast actually waved his coat from the top of one of the stands.'

Two days after the match, Lord Harris dispatched another letter to the Lancashire committee on the subject of 'unfair bowling'. And for the first time Lord Harris named names, asserting that Crossland 'was bowling as unfairly as ever'.

In an extremely lengthy missive, Lord Harris eventually came to the point, which was that the return fixture, scheduled for Tonbridge in August, would be cancelled and Lancashire would be awarded the match 'by default'.

Swire replied that the actions of neither Crossland nor Nash had been questioned by 'any of the most competent umpires in the country'. He added that the committee had full confidence in their captain, A.N.Hornby.

Swire told Lord Harris that a copy of the correspondence had been forwarded to the MCC committee, but the Lancashire secretary could have saved himself a lot of trouble – and ink – for Crossland had already played his last game for the county. It was against Cheshire in a non-Championship fixture at Cale Park, Stockport on June 26 and 27, where he signed off with figures of two for 19 and three for 38.

In fact, on the same day Swire was penning his letter, the MCC committee had decided that Crossland no longer possessed the necessary residential qualification to play for Lancashire. MCC gathered together what might have been the cast of an Agatha Christie novel, including rate and rent collectors, a village policeman and a country squire, and they gave evidence that Crossland had lived in his native county, Nottinghamshire, from October 1884 to April 1885.

At about the same time, Nash was no longer a regular member of the Lancashire side. He played in only 54 matches for the county and by 1885 he had joined the Darlington club and the following year joined Leyland, where he remained for nine years. He returned to the county of his birth Buckinghamshire, playing for them from 1894 until 1903, the year of his death at the age of 53.

In the same season, 1882, that Lord Harris first pointed the finger at Crossland and Nash, he had clashed with Lancashire over the eligibility of Sandford Schultz. Schultz had toured Australia with Harris in 1878/9, and was due to play for Lancashire against Kent at Old Trafford in mid-June of that year.

When Harris heard that Schultz, who was born at Birkenhead in Cheshire, was in the home eleven, he wired Old Trafford that he was 'surprised' that he had been chosen as he understood he 'had no qualification'. On arriving at the ground, Lord Harris confronted Hornby and Edmund Rowley. Once again Hornby vehemently defended his player, claiming that Schultz was qualified to play for Lancashire as he had, in fact, been born in the Port of Liverpool.

For once, Harris was stunned into silence, although in truth he was correct, as Schultz well knew: he had given Birkenhead as his birthplace on the 1881 census. The production of a birth certificate would have been enough to settle the issue; but Schultz was a member of the Stock Exchange, whose motto is *Dictum Meum Pactum* (My word is my bond).

Schultz made nine appearances for Lancashire and also turned out for Huntingdonshire and Lincolnshire. He changed his surname from the Germanic-sounding Schultz to Storey as a result of anti-German feeling during the First World War.

Ironically, after his disqualification Crossland settled in Lancashire, living for a time at Clayton-le-Moors and also in Blackburn. He worked as a general labourer and later as a railway fish porter but continued to play cricket, appearing for Hornby's old club, East Lancashire, Blackburn, Church, Oswaldtwistle and Colne. When he died at the age of 51 he was buried at Blackburn with his funeral expenses being paid for by Lancashire – a sad postscript to a sad story.

Even with the throwing controversy settled, albeit unsatisfactorily, Kent and Lancashire did not meet at Tonbridge that August.

With Crossland banned and Nash no longer around, Hornby was delighted that Lancashire were able to unearth another bowler, the slow left-armer, Johnny Briggs, who turned out to be one of the greatest in the club's history.

But while Briggs was a straight swap for Nash as it were, there was still a fast-bowling vacancy to be filled. In stepped a remarkable character, Bennett Hudson, who Lancashire hoped would fit the bill. Hudson was a Yorkshireman with long experience of league cricket and qualified for Lancashire by virtue of his engagement as a professional with Bacup and Longsight. The Sheffield-born man had played three matches for Yorkshire without much success. He scored a handful of runs and didn't bowl in any of his games for the White Rose county so it must have required a giant leap of faith, mixed with a hint of desperation, for Lancashire to take him on six years after his final Yorkshire appearance.

But he duly made an impressive debut in the 1886 season – although he excelled with the bat and not the ball. He scored 98 against Sussex followed by 85 against Oxford University, a whirlwind innings that contained sixteen boundaries. Hornby was so excited by this performance that he awarded Hudson his county cap, hurling the coveted head gear through the pavilion window!

Unfortunately, Hudson's bowling didn't impress Hornby or the Lancashire committee and after five games, in which he managed only three wickets, he returned from whence he came, playing regularly in league cricket for Burnley between 1887 and 1890.

Arthur Mold

When he felt the opposition was bending the rules, Hornby was never slow to react. It usually took the form of refusing to carry on with the game. There was one such a moment in the game against Essex at Leyton in August 1897. The two counties had previously played six friendly games and one first-class one, all of which Lancashire had won, but this was the first time they had met in a first-class match at Leyton. Both teams were Championship contenders and Essex believed that Lancashire fast bowler Arthur Mold, who played a major role in their defeat at Old Trafford earlier in the season, had an unfair action. One could sense there was tension in the air.

Arthur Mold. 'He was one of the deadliest fast bowlers of his day, but right through his career the fairness of his delivery formed the subject of lively discussion.' – Wisden obituary by Sydney Pardon

The incident involved Mold, who was batting and Frederick Bull, an amateur off-break bowler who was also Essex's assistant secretary. Lancashire were in trouble on a wearing wicket, but when it looked likely that Lancashire would be following on, Bull made every effort to ensure that Essex would not have to bat last. Bull bowled one wide, which went to the boundary, but Mold called his bluff and proceeded to hit his own wicket so that Lancashire did have to go in again. Mold's decision to sacrifice his wicket gave Bull figures of seven for 63. There was a heated discussion among the players at the interval and Hornby said he was refusing to proceed with the game. Each side accused the other of sharp practice but once Bull apologised for deliberately bowling wide, the game continued.

Later Hornby managed to defend and criticise Mold at the same time when he said: 'I have been connected with first-class cricket over thirty years and have never seen such a disgraceful thing in connection with the game. Indeed, I was completely amazed when I saw Mold had knocked his wicket down and could hardly believe it, but when I heard the explanation and Bull admitted what he done and apologised to me, I could not blame my men. But it is not my idea of playing cricket. Under the circumstances, which I hope will not occur again whilst I am playing cricket, I think Mold was justified in his action although personally I should never agree to anything of that sort being done.'

Mold's tactics didn't work, Essex winning by six wickets to go top of the table for the first time in their history, although it was Lancashire who went on to win the Championship.

Ironically, Frederick Bull's action also came under scrutiny and he dropped out of the first-class game as a result of the crackdown on throwing. He later took a commercial appointment in Blackburn before turning professional. He played for the East Lancashire club among others, but after the 1910 season he took his own life.

Although the Crossland and Nash matter was closed, Lancashire and Hornby were to run into another maelstrom of controversy in June 1900 when Mold was called for throwing by umpire James Phillips in the game against Nottinghamshire at Trent Bridge. Phillips had called Mold from square-leg in what was the first season that square-leg umpires were authorised to call no-balls when they thought a bowler was throwing.

There is a remarkable film of Hornby and Mold, who was again no-balled 16 times in 10 overs (although the film voice-over states that he was no-balled 15 times) by Phillips in the match against Somerset at Old Trafford in July 1901. Initially, he was called by Phillips from square leg, but when Mold changed ends, Phillips continued to no-ball him from the bowler's end.

The film forms part of a unique record of Edwardian England provided by Sagar Mitchell and James Kenyon and which is now known as the Mitchell and Kenyon Collection. The films were found in the basement of a shop in Blackburn, (Hornby's birthplace) and restored by the British Film Institute.

The Mold controversy was a big story in its day and Mitchell and Kenyon were there to capture some of the drama. The film, which can be seen on the eponymous YouTube website, lasts for eight

English umpires were ex-professional cricketers and even the best of them tended to be subservient to the amateurs. James Phillips, an Australian, had no such qualms, and as early as 1898 was not afraid to no ball that ultimate Corinthian, C.B.Fry.

minutes and 42 seconds with a commentary by the TV personality Adrian Chiles, and Hornby's appearance is crucial to the storyline.

Hornby is seen in the nets facing Mold's bowling. He cuts a rather portly figure – as does Mold – a far cry from the super-fit athletes of today. Mold's action is very much round-arm – in the style of Sri Lanka's Lasith Malinga, often referred to as 'Malinga the Slinger' but who has never been called for throwing. The choice of Hornby to face Mold's bowling was a deliberate ploy by Lancashire. It was thought that Hornby's impeccable reputation at both county and international level would help to ensure that the good name of Lancashire cricket would remain untainted.

Archie MacLaren, who was captaining Lancashire in the match in question, said later that he kept Mold on – even though he had been no-balled – at the insistence of Hornby, who was presumably keen to prove a point. Phillips' actions didn't seem to faze Mold who took three for 88 and four for 65 as he helped the home side to a ten-wicket win. Mold reached 50 wickets for the season with his second dismissal of the match.

But Mold's career was irreparably damaged and he played only a handful of games for Lancashire after the Somerset match, taking just four more first-class wickets, before slipping into minor league cricket. He eventually became a publican in his native Northamptonshire, which he combined with looking after his elderly mother.

Hornby, described by Chiles as 'a true Corinthian and brilliant captain', is seen batting in the nets with pads but without gloves. He looks every bit as aggressive as his reputation suggested although it must be said that his style was more rudimentary than classical. However, his figures suggest it was none the less extremely effective.

There is no actual footage of any play during the game against Somerset but there is plenty of coverage of the players taking the field and coming off. The opening scene is notable for a steam train chugging past the ground evoking memories of a bygone era.

At the time of writing, the YouTube film had already had over 11,700 views. It portrays a cricketing era we will never see again, and I highly recommend it. The film was also shown on BBC Four during its Mitchell and Kenyon series, first shown in 2007 and again in 2011.

One assumes that the Mitchell and Kenyon film was the same one shown at St James's Theatre and Exhibition Hall in Manchester on the Saturday night following the Somerset fixture. Among those in the 'immense gathering' that evening were Mold, MacLaren and other cricketers.

Chapter Nine
The hand of Hornby?

It is necessary to say quite plainly that I attribute our failure this season very largely to the unfortunate policy the committee are pursuing - Albert Henry Hornby on the Lancashire committee

Throughout his life, Hornby never ran away from a fight or from an opportunity to stand up for those who played or served under him.

And, sometimes, Hornby would instigate a confrontation. But it was his son Albert Henry who was at the forefront of controversy when he gave an inflammatory statement to a *Manchester Guardian* reporter towards the end of the 1913 county season.

Like his father, A.H. attended Harrow and, according to *Cambridge University Alumni 1261-1900*, failed to complete his degree - in his case at Trinity College. In 1902/3 he toured India with a team called the Oxford University Authentics which, as he was a Cambridge man, seems far from authentic.

The censuses of 1901 and 1911 show him 'living on own means' at Parkfield with his parents. He was still there in 1925, although by then he had married Esmé Lonsdale, with whom he had three children.

A.H. made his Lancashire debut in 1899 and played in his father's last Championship match at Grace Road, Leicester, in which A.N. scored 53 and captained Lancashire to a huge win by an innings and 170 runs.

A.H. became a regular in the side from 1903, and took on the captaincy in 1908. He finished with a career average of 24.58, slightly higher than his father's 24.07, although pitches in A.H.'s day were probably better.

In 1909, father and son found themselves on opposite sides when the 62-year-old A.N. captained a team of 23 Lancashire Colts against a 12-man Lancashire side led by A.H. Despite A.N.'s bold second innings declaration when the Colts were only 12 wickets down, the match ended in a draw.

At the time of the newspaper interview A.H. was just completing his fifth season as captain and might have been expected to keep any issues he might have had 'in house'. But Albert Henry was certainly a chip off the old block and many detected the hand of his father in the way his son made his feelings so public.

COUNTY CRICKETERS.

MR. A. H. HORNBY.
LANCASHIRE.

'A chip off the old block.' A.N.'s son, Albert Henry, was one of his successors as captain, and a capable cricketer in his own right.

Hornby the Younger's complaints were, in the main, down to money.

Towards the end of a poor season when the side won only seven of their Championship games, drawing eight and losing eleven, Hornby put the blame firmly on the Lancashire committee, of which he was a co-opted member.

He told the *Manchester Guardian*'s representative that any team had to be in a contented and united frame of mind in order to perform to the best of its ability.

Among his bones of contention were the fact that the committee intended to cut down on expenses by discontinuing a travelling saloon and a lunch for players for long journeys for the following season; stopping salaries when players were unable to play through illness, overwork or injury; and limiting talent money.

The captain was also concerned that the committee was proposing to reduce next year's programme when they were, in fact, canvassing for more members; depriving young players on the staff of match practice and not encouraging coming men of the stamp of William and James Tyldesley.

Hornby also felt that there was a lack of committee men taking a personal interest in the players.

Summing up Albert Henry pulled no punches: 'It is necessary to say quite plainly that I attribute our failure this season very largely to the unfortunate policy the committee are pursuing.'

This was a devastating critique of the Lancashire committee made all the more so because it was now very firmly in the public domain.

But it was no surprise that Albert Henry's father A.N. fully endorsed his son's remarks.

Another to offer his support was John J Bentley, who for a short time was manager of Manchester United and who had been a county member for many years.

Many members felt that Hornby had been right to speak out, while others felt that his statement was a 'letter of resignation' from the captaincy.

A meeting of members, chaired by Sir Arthur Howarth, was convened to discuss Hornby's claims. Hornby himself was greeted with cheers when he spoke and there were cries of dissent from the packed audience when he offered to resign the captaincy, but the get-together left the whole issue in abeyance. One newspaper report described the meeting as having come to 'a quiet and inconclusive end'.

Interestingly, Hornby senior kept his distance. He did not attend the meeting and a few Lancashire members commented that he should have been present to try to heal the rift that his son had opened up.

Subsequently, Hornby Jnr was to lead the side in the following season, during which the team posted a similar record to 1913 with six wins, eleven draws and nine defeats in their 26 matches. It was his last season as Lancashire skipper.

Cricinfo, normally a reliable source, records in an article published on its website on 21 August 2009, that

> Monkey Hornby was called from the field when he was captaining Lancashire against Yorkshire (at Old Trafford in August 1914) and summoned to the War Office, and within hours Sir Archibald White, Yorkshire's skipper was heading

south to join his regiment. The following evening war was declared against Germany, and within 48 hours a number of other players, including Pelham Warner, Middlesex's captain, and Arthur Carr, Nottinghamshire's skipper, abandoned their cricket commitments and headed off to war.

But A.N. was not captaining Lancashire in this match – Reggie Spooner led the team – and he didn't play for the county after 1906.

Cricinfo got its Hornbys in a twist – the Hornby called away to advise the War Office was Albert Henry, the Lancashire captain. He was unable to play in the Roses match at Old Trafford, which began on 3 August 1914, and had, in fact, already played his last game for Lancashire. A fine horseman just like his father, A.H. was required to advise the War Office on the subject of horses for the cavalry, and served as a Captain in the Remount Services throughout the war. *War Horse*, the book by Michael Morpurgo, which became a hit on the West End stage and was subsequently filmed by Steven Spielberg, gives some idea of what this would have entailed.

Britain declared war on Germany on the second day of the match. In common with most counties Lancashire played their remaining fixtures – three at home and four away – after MCC issued a statement saying that no good purpose could be served by abandoning games. But there was no more Championship cricket played in the country until 1919.

Hornby senior was present, along with a number of other greats from the past, when Lancashire resumed Championship duties on Monday 19 May 1919. He was among a small crowd for the opening day against Northamptonshire that welcomed cricket back. Sadly, Lancashire's opening batsmen, Harold Garnett and Bill Tyldesley, had died in the conflict, while the visitors' openers, brothers Arthur and Bill Denton, had both been prisoners of war. Lancashire seemed to realise that the crowd, starved of sporting action for so long, wanted to see something special – and they didn't let the spectators down, scoring 200 in 135 minutes with the *Manchester Evening News* reporting 'that the batsmen were living up to the spirit of the new times'.

Chapter Ten
A Lancashire legend is laid to rest

The spirit of the game has never been warmer and more lovable than it was when the breeze that was Hornby blew over Old Trafford – Manchester Guardian obituary

Hornby visited Old Trafford for the opening match of the 1924 season against Derbyshire, sitting in an invalid chair by the side of the pitch. Well wrapped up, and wearing a hat with Lancashire's colours on it, to counter the early-season chill, he was back at the scene of some of his greatest triumphs. In his youth he had rarely worn a cap as he scampered singles, re-arranged his field or showed his prowess in the deep, taking countless catches.

But now, 76 years of age, and almost immobile, he cut a disconsolate figure.

It was to be his last visit to Old Trafford and nineteen months later – on 17 December 1925 – Hornby passed away at the age of 78 at his home in Parkfield. The cause of death was given as 'senile decay' and 'cardiac failure'. But the *Nantwich Chronicle* decided that 'Mr Hornby just fell asleep'.

So three weeks after the Lancashire annual meeting, the man who had steered the course of the county's cricket for five decades, was dead.

The cortege left Parkfield, watched by two of Hornby's horses, as it wended its way to Acton Parish Church, followed by a lengthy procession of cars.

According to the *Liverpool Banner* 'the crowd was so large that only mourners, personal and hunting friends, deputations of cricketers and civic bodies were able to find room in the church during the first part of the funeral service'.

The mourners, standing bare-headed in the rain, overflowed into the churchyard during the church service, and later, crowded round the graveside where the committal service was recited by a former Rugby international, the Reverend F.O.Poole. It was a case of Ashes to ashes as Hornby was laid to rest.

A mass of wreaths were piled high on the grass surrounding the grave with one of the most prominent from Lancashire consisting of red roses. Other floral tributes came from the MCC, Middlesex, Yorkshire and Surrey, from the Rugby Football Union and the Nantwich cricket and football clubs.

In a moving moment, Hornby's son Albert Henry plucked a red rose from the Lancashire wreath and threw it into the grave.

In his final years Hornby was wracked by pain and he must have been terribly frustrated by both his inability to get around under his own steam and by the waning of his mental capabilities.

Writer Neville Cardus had tried to interview Hornby a few years before his death and later wrote that 'the old gentleman' did not respond to his questions about past exploits and that he had been unable to unlock his memory.

But Hornby was nothing if not a fighter and even in death he had the better of two of his most famous contemporaries, surviving both Barlow, who had died in Blackpool in 1919, and Grace, who passed away four years earlier.

Three Lancashire captains: A.N.Hornby, Miles Kenyon, A.C.MacLaren.

*Barlow had designed his own headstone which featured a broken wicket
(above), but Hornby's memorial left the stumps undisturbed.*

The grave at Acton had already received the body of his son, Walter Ingram and eventually his wife, Ada Sarah (1927), his daughter-in-law Henrietta (1961) and granddaughter Georgie in 1990. Although the inscription on the gravestone makes reference to John and George Vernon, their bodies lie in Canada and South Africa respectively. Hornby's oldest son, Albert Henry, was buried at North Kilworth in Leicestershire along with his wife, Esmé Lonsdale. According to the churchwarden at Acton the plot is now closed.

The obituaries flowed like runs from Hornby's bat with the *Manchester Guardian* leading the way on 18 December 1925:

> Hornby's virtue, especially as a batsman, was a passion for taking a risk.
> Though he was probably as clever technically as most of the modern masters, skill was not enough for the expression of his vigorous spirit.
> When Hornby was at the wicket nobody could be certain what was about to happen; the one thing we could be pretty sure was, sooner or later, Barlow would be run out.
> Hornby played on wickets that were continually springing their surprise into the game; now a good length ball would shoot along the grass and now it would 'kick' chest high.
> The cricket of Hornby's period was not only a thing that compelled admiration and excitement but it also compelled laughter.

Later in the obituary, the Guardian painted this evocative picture of Hornby's batting style:

> Hornby at the wicket went after a ball rather as he went at a dangerous ditch in the hunting field.
> Much has come into cricket since Hornby's day – a more ordered and extensive technique. But the spirit of the game has never been warmer and more lovable than it was when the breeze that was Hornby blew over Old Trafford.

Hornby's obit in the 1926 edition of *Wisden* recalls that:

> Hornby in playing Spofforth [in the MCC match against Australia in 1878] met with an injury of so severe a description that it compelled his retirement and would certainly have kept most men out of the field for a week or so, but such was his indomitable pluck that with his side faring disastrously – they were all out for 19 – he came [back] to resume his innings.

The painful experience, however, shook even his splendid nerve, for, although he remained one of England's leading batsmen for several years after, his only score against Spofforth was one of 94 for the North in 1884.

Earlier in the obituary *Wisden* describes Hornby thus:

For many seasons one of the leading England batsmen, Hornby had an attractive forward style and possessed splendid, punishing powers which he used freely.

In addition, he was a magnificent field, and as a captain so firm, keen and genial that he could always get the best out of the men under his charge.

His dashing methods, coupled with his obvious enthusiasm – he appeared to thoroughly enjoy every moment he was on the field – made him a general favourite wherever he went.

Chapter Eleven
What are we to make of him?

No skipper was so genuinely appreciative of good work on the part of his men or so fearless in his unstinting efforts to win the game – A.C.MacLaren on Hornby

As everyone is aware there are 'lies, damned lies and statistics' and I accept that figures can be manipulated to give an often misleading impression. Spin doctors – and I don't mean the likes of Shane Warne and Muttiah Muralitharan – have been subtly adjusting figures to suit their political needs for many years. But cricket statistics, more than those for any other sport, more often than not give a true reflection of a player's worth, particularly when the 'sample' is a large one.

Of course, with most leading proponents of the game the final figures are garnered from a high number of appearances and that is certainly the case with Hornby. After all, his career spanned almost 33 years, 437 first-class matches and three Tests.

Admittedly, he was singularly unsuccessful in those three games at international level, but in first-class games he compiled 16 centuries and 74 half-centuries for a highly respectable average of 24.07, taking into account the uncovered and often largely untreated pitches prevalent in the era during which Hornby operated.

For Lancashire, he made 292 appearances, his average rising slightly to 24.25. By contrast the obdurate Dick Barlow played 249 times for Lancashire for an average of 20.43. It was a measure of his importance to the county that between 1870 and 1881 no Lancashire batsman made a century apart from Hornby, who reached three figures on seven occasions in that period.

Hornby reached his zenith as a batsman in 1881 when his 1,534 runs included three tons. Twice in that year Hornby scored more runs in a single knock than Lancashire's opponents did in two completed innings. The first instance occurred when he hit his highest first-class score, 188, against Derbyshire at Old Trafford in May. The visitors replied with all-out totals of 102 and 62 –

24 short of Hornby's contribution. Derbyshire were again on the receiving end at Derby two months later when Hornby made 145 and the home side was dismissed for 48 and 59, a shortfall of 38 measured against Hornby's effort.

Hornby made the bulk of his runs before 1890 batting mainly as an opener, but post-1890 he was content to drop himself down the order to give other batsmen in the side a better opportunity, with the result that his average fell away somewhat. He certainly wasn't interested in plumping up his average like a farmer might fatten a turkey for the Christmas market.

He was also a remarkably good fielder with a total of 313 catches and occasionally kept wicket.

Never a publication to damn anyone with faint praise, *Wisden* gave its considered opinion on Hornby's career in its edition of 1901:

> The season was memorable (also) for being the first for more than thirty years in which the name of A.N.Hornby did not once figure as one of the Lancashire batsmen.
>
> At the age of fifty-three, it is not surprising that Mr Hornby has thought fit to cease active participation in county cricket but all the same it is a matter for regret that the career of so great a batsman should have come to an end.
>
> What he did for Lancashire for a quarter of a century, both as a batsman and captain, could not very well be overpraised. His determined hitting won many a match for his side, and in the matter of leadership and management of men, he has had no superior for many a long day.
>
> Happily, his health is still of the best and his interest in the game in which he has borne so famous a part remains unabated.

That respected observer of Lancashire cricket, Brian Bearshaw, who covered the county scene for more than 25 years (although not in Hornby's era) suggested that Hornby 'proved to be the single most influential person in the history of Lancashire County Cricket Club. He transformed Lancashire into a formidable side and was captain when they won the Championship in 1881 and 1897'. Few will wish to argue with that considered assessment.

Even Kent's Lord Harris, one of his greatest rivals and a key figure in the throwing controversy that engulfed the two clubs, had this to say on learning of Hornby's passing: 'I suppose what he did for Lancashire only Lancashire people know, but it was evident to everybody outside Lancashire that he was the soul of that club.'

Author and cricket historian Eric Midwinter summed up his captaincy in these well-chosen words:

> He was one of the first cricket captains to think collectively and gather his players into a team.
> The parts fitted together and worked hard for each other, their fielding strength being an indicative token of that togetherness.
> He proved to be a well-informed and cunning leader, not only capable of building and moulding his colleagues into a superior outfit, but of assiduously sapping at the weak linkages of his opponents.

So how does one summarise the career of a man for whom the phrase multi-faceted might have been coined? After all, Hornby was one of the great batsmen of his era and captained England in two Tests and played in one other. It was considered by many that his only superior as a batsman in this period was the legendary W.G.Grace.

An astute and often inspirational captain of Lancashire for 20 years, he demanded – and received – the utmost loyalty from all who played under him. In all, he played for the Red Rose county for almost 33 years. He led Lancashire in 232 of his 292 games for them.

His bowling, however, never reached anywhere near Grace's heights. The bearded wonder claimed 2,809 wickets in 870 first-class appearances, while Hornby, bowling left- and right-handed underarm deliveries harvested just eleven wickets in his 437 first-class matches.

Off the field he was president of Lancashire for 22 years and served as chairman for a further 20 years, bringing his association with Lancashire to a remarkable 49 years. It's an unbroken span of service that will never be beaten.

However, there was a surprising challenge to Hornby's presidency at the annual meeting of December 1907. It was pointed out, respectfully of course, that success in a playing capacity didn't always translate itself to an off-field role. There were also grumblings about the state of the finances, the decline in the number of members and the loss of the club's better players. But the committee wouldn't support the move and the resolution was withdrawn. Despite the resolution's withdrawal, within ten years the club had decided that presidents could only stay in office for two years. In the event it meant that President Hornby had served ten times as long as such luminaries as Lord Derby, Sir Edwin Stockton, Lord Stanley, Sir Edward Rhodes, Rev Canon F Paton-Williams, Sir Neville Cardus and Brian Statham although a number of them served two separate terms.

Of course, Hornby wasn't everyone's cup of tea. As C.G.Howard, who served as secretary of Lancashire from 1949-1965, wrote in *Lancashire County Cricket 100 Years of Cricket*: 'He ruled with a generally benevolent despotism both on and off the field.'

Hornby played nine times for England at Rugby at three-quarter and full-back, captaining the side on one occasion, and football for Blackburn Rovers. He was a keen boxer and sparred with world champion Jem Mace in Australia; he was a top-class hurdler even showing off his skills aboard the *S.S.Sarmatian* en route to North America. And he rode to hounds regularly with his own stable of hunters and was a regular, if sometimes erratic, shot.

From a wealthy family background in an era when fast-developing, industrial Lancashire was a mixture of immense riches and dire poverty, Hornby was lucky enough to be able to play as a genuine amateur throughout his career.

Later in life he recognised that the distinction between amateurs and professionals was becoming a little blurred so that when Jack Sharp, a former professional-turned-amateur, was appointed Lancashire captain in 1923, Hornby wrote: 'Dear Sharp, Wishing you all the very best this coming season. No good my saying "play up Lancashire" because they always did and always will do. Yours ever. A.N.Hornby.' It was a change of tune from Hornby, who years earlier, had treated with scorn the idea of any professional – or former professional – captaining the side.

Sharp was too ill to play in several of the opening Championship games in his first season as captain, so Lancashire persuaded 49-year-old J.T. (Johnny) Tyldesley to forsake his coaching and second team duties to lead the side in the Whitsuntide clash against Yorkshire at Old Trafford. Unfortunately, Hornby's thoughts on this matter are not recorded. Although a professional throughout his great career, Tyldesley, who scored almost 32,000 runs in 507 Lancashire games and played 31 Tests for England, captained the team as an amateur. It was his only appearance of the season.

But although sometimes aloof and often harsh, Hornby was fiercely committed to his players. His defence of the suspect bowling actions of Arthur Mold, John Crossland and George Nash

In 1997 this blue plaque was unveiled at Brook House to mark the 150th anniversary of Hornby's birth, and his achievements as a sportsman.

was testament to this quality and it was mirrored in the 1930s by Arthur Carr, the Nottinghamshire and England skipper, who stood firmly behind Harold Larwood and Bill Voce during the 'Bodyline' controversy – a stance which eventually cost him the county captaincy.

Like Carr, Hornby demanded equally fierce loyalty from those who played under him and he was quick to admonish players he thought weren't pulling their weight.

In a time when men were expected to keep their emotions tightly under control, Hornby wore his heart on the sleeve of his cricket shirt and a number of forays into the crowd when he felt spectators were getting out of hand underlined his passion. He was also keen to take up the cudgels when he felt he was being unfairly criticised by the gentlemen of the press and, on occasions, he could be seen chasing a cricket writer out of the ground at Old Trafford when he felt he had been wronged in print. Today Hornby would have been the darling of the tabloids.

Of course, Hornby was privileged enough to be able to devote most of his life to his sporting endeavours – and to Lancashire cricket in particular. But one must never forget how much time and effort he did expend in the cause of Lancashire cricket.

That he never replicated his county form for England is a big disappointment and there were some Australian pundits who felt he wasn't good enough to represent his country in any case.

His England failures must have hurt Hornby deeply. One by-product was that the defeat at The Oval, over which he presided in 1882, begat the Ashes. For that he will, somewhat unfairly in my opinion, always be remembered.

But it didn't damage Hornby's cricketing career as a whole. He gave so much more to the game of cricket in five decades of unpaid endeavour. For that alone, cricket-lovers, especially those who have Lancashire's interests at heart, owe Hornby an enormous debt of gratitude.

The Record That Never Was, and Other Fascinating Facts

AT one time Hornby was in the *Guinness Book of Records* for scoring the most runs – ten – off a single ball. But it never happened. The story retailed in a contemporaneous newspaper report said the incident occurred when he was facing James Street in the Surrey v Lancashire match at The Oval in July 1873. It was repeated by no less a statistical guru than Bill Frindall. In fact, Hornby actually scored ten in one four-ball over with four, nought, two and four.

Just to clear up the matter once and for all, I reproduce a letter, written by the cricket author Gerald Brodribb, from the Spring 1994 issue of *The Cricket Statistician*, which appeared under the heading, *The Hornby Hit*. Brodribb wrote:

> I first became aware of this alleged hit for 'ten' in Frindall's 1986 edition of *Cricket Record*s page 146. I then looked up *Bell's Life* for an account of this match: Lancashire v Surrey at The Oval, July 14, 15, 16, 1873.

> A quote from *Bell's Life* reads: 'Street bowled the second over. Mr Hornby dashed away at Street's first delivery, making no less than ten runs from it.' That's all. There was no mention of such a hit in *James Lillywhite's Cricketers Annual* ['Red Lilly'] for 1874, page 69. The match scores were: Lancashire 100 and 115, Surrey 33 and 76. Rain affected conditions for Surrey.

> The next thing to do was to look up the actual scorebook. I found this at Old Trafford. Hornby's scores were:
> 1st innings 20 1,4,2,4,2,1,1,3,2
> 2nd innings 13 2,3,2,1,2,3

> I can only suggest that the ten in *Bell's Life* was an error for four and the comments 'no less than' suggests that it was either a rare boundary hit, or an all-run hit for four.

> All this shows how necessary it is to check original scorebooks (wherever possible).

The Cricket Statistician's editor, Philip Bailey, commented that perhaps the ten runs comprised the separate shots 4, 2, 4 off Street's over.

The ten-off-a-ball feat was achieved 27 years later, in May 1900, by Samuel Wood off Cuthbert James Burnup for Derbyshire against the MCC at Lord's. Wood's achievement is mentioned in *The Ultimate Cricket Fact and Quiz Book*, which was published in 1999, and was at one time included in the *Guinness Book of Records*.

Wood was helped by the use of netting, which was brought in by MCC and abandoned after a short trial. It was described as a 'perverse reward system' by Andrew Ward in *Cricket's Strangest Matches* published in 1990. If a batsman hit the ball into the netting it might have been possible to run ten as in those days fielders had only moderate long-throwing ability. It is conceivable that, if they thought the ball was going for four, they might amble to the boundary to collect it, whereupon it might have been caught up in the netting and by the time they eventually reached it the batsmen might have run eight, nine or ten.

Wood was plain unvarnished Wood until changing his name to Hill-Wood by Royal Consent in 1912. He had a baronetcy conferred on him in 1941 and four of his sons played for Derbyshire. One, Wilfred William was known as Whisky and Water, while another, BS, was nicknamed Brandy and Soda, according to *The Official History of Derbyshire Cricket Club* by John Shawcroft.

Roy Webber's *The Book of Cricket Records* (1961 revised edition) states that there have been nine instances of batsmen scoring nine off one delivery between 1841 and 1946, which, of course, covers the Hornby era.

Hornby did manage eight off one ball, including four overthrows, playing for MCC against Derbyshire at Lord's in June 1885.

*****

HORNBY was involved in some strange goings-on when playing for the United South of England against Twenty-Two of Stockport at Cale Green, Stockport, which began on August 31, 1876. For a start the game was originally scheduled for two days but was extended to three. The *Stockport Advertiser* reported that W.G.Grace, opening the batting for the United South team, retired hurt without scoring after suffering a split finger. On the final day Grace was seemingly over his injury problem, but had made only 13 in the visitors' second innings before he was caught off the bowling of Barks by Thomas Whatmough, the Stockport professional who appeared twice for Lancashire. Grace, however, was allowed to come in again when the United South team had reached 77 for eight. The newspaper added that the crowd, reckoned to be 6,000-plus, 'showed their appreciation [of the decision] by a hearty round of applause'. Stockport managed to grass Grace four times as he went on to compile 133. Basically, the game finished when Grace was finally out.

It is not known whether Hornby was captaining the local team although he may well have been and would, therefore, have been complicit in allowing Grace's return to the crease.

*****

QUICK finishes appeared to be a Hornby speciality as he played in five matches scheduled for three days which ended in one. Interestingly, four of the games were played in the month of May. The matches were Oxford University v MCC at Magdalen Ground, Oxford in May 1877; MCC v Australians at Lord's in May 1878; MCC v Lancashire at Lord's in May 1886 (the game ended on the second day after no play was possible on the first); North v South at Lord's in May 1887; and Lancashire v Surrey at Old Trafford in August 1888. However, Hornby missed out on playing in two other one-day finishes, the Lancashire v Somerset fixtures of 1892 and 1894.

The first of those matches produced the joint lowest all-out total in first class-cricket. In 1877 Oxford University managed just 12 in their first innings, with only seven scoring shots. In defence of the students, six of them were making their first-class debuts, while another failed to turn up in time to bat in the innings although he opened in the second innings. Hornby and his opening partner, Isaac Walker, put on 51 for MCC's first wicket, four more than the university side managed in their two completed innings. The game, scheduled for three days, was over on the first day. Northamptonshire gained an unwanted share of the record when they were also dismissed for 12 by Gloucestershire in 1907.

*****

HORNBY played in one tied match, the Gentlemen v Players fixture at The Oval in June 1883, but missed the Surrey v Lancashire match of 1894 that also ended in a tie.

*****

HORNBY scored 79 per cent of the runs for MCC in their first innings against Sussex at Lord's in May 1890, with 45 out of 57 in a match during which 36 wickets fell in four hours. Sussex won by four wickets.

*****

LIKE many sportsmen and women, Hornby was superstitious. Once, when going out to open the innings, he noticed that he had put his pads on the wrong legs. He returned to the pavilion, where he told his team-mates: 'I'm going in last instead of first. If I went in now I should have the bad luck to get somebody else or myself out without scoring!'

*****

HORNBY'S brother-in-law Walter Herbert Ingram was a soldier of fortune who is probably best remembered as a soldier of misfortune. He is said to have met a tragic end, at the age of 33, as the result of the Mummy's Curse, which affected 20 people who are alleged to have died through suicide, accidents and exotic diseases after disturbing the tombs of ancient Egyptian kings in the 1920s.

Ingram joined the Gordon Relief Expedition in Egypt in 1885, the doomed military operation to rescue General Gordon from an Islamic uprising at Khartoum.

The mission failed but Ingram fought heroically on the front line and escaped with his life. On his way home he bought a mummy case, which was said to have a fearful inscription cursing anyone who might disturb it. Three years later Ingram was trampled to death by a wounded elephant about 40 miles from the city of Berbera in Somaliland. Because of his family involvement with the *Illustrated London News*, the news of Ingram's death gained widespread coverage, not least in the *ILN* itself. Rudyard Kipling also heard the tragic tale and relayed it to his friend and fellow-writer Rider Haggard.

*****

THERE is even a Facebook page devoted to Hornby, which states that 'to interact with A.N.Hornby you need to sign up for Facebook first'. It doesn't, however, explain what form that interaction might take!

*****

*Like Hornby, the Sussex and England Women's slow left-arm bowler
Holly Colvin has the nickname 'Monkey'.*

Acknowledgments

I would like to thank the following people, without whom this book would not have been possible: Stephen Williams for undertaking an enormous amount of the research, mainly through his own superb cricketing library, and for reading the first draft; ACS members David Jeater, who was a great source of encouragement; David Pracy, who did a truly marvellous job as my editor, was never short of constructive ideas and comments, and has made the book a much better read than it otherwise would have been; Martin Tebay of Red Rose Books; Malcolm Lorimer, the Lancashire chaplain and archivist; Peter Wall, whose unpublished work on Hornby is truly a labour of love; the late Don Ambrose; Keith Hayhurst; Georgina Hoole; Philip Paine; Tony Martin; Pat Jeater; Eric Greenwood, East Lancashire CC club historian and statistician; Chris Punchard of Maldon CC and Steven Sheen.

The images on pages 17-26 and page 101 are © Blackburn with Darwen Library and Information Services and taken from their website at www.cottontown.org

The images on pages 5, 31, 56, 77, 84 and 86 are from the Roger Mann Collection and those on pages 4, 42, 49, 69, 70, 73 and 79 from Lancashire County Cricket Club.

I am grateful to everyone who has kindly given permission to reproduce images and particularly to the above three.

Dedication

Last, but by no means least, a special word of thanks to my wife Bella, who put up with my long hours hogging the computer, both early in the morning and late at night. I would like, therefore, to dedicate this book to her and our four cricket-loving children, Alex, Oscar, Edgar and Edward.

Edgware, London
January 2013

Bibliography

Books

W.A.Abram, *Members of the Hornby Family who have Represented
   Blackburn in Parliament*, George Falkner & Sons 1892

David Rayvern Allen, *A Song for Cricket*, Pelham Books 1981

David Rayvern Allen [ed], *Cricket's Silver Lining 1864-1914*,
   Guild Publishing 1987

David Rayvern Allen, *Cricket with Grace*, Unwin Hyman 1990

Philip Bailey, Philip Thorn, Peter Wynne-Thomas, *Who's Who of Cricketers*
   (revised and updated edition 1993), published
   in association with the ACS

R G Barlow, *Forty Seasons of First-Class Cricket*, re-printed by
   Red Rose Books 2002

Brian Bearshaw, *From the Stretford End*, Partridge Press 1990

Derek Birley, *A Social History of English Cricket*, Aurum Press 1999

Gerald Brodribb, *The Lost Art: A History of Underarm Bowling*,
   Boundary Books 1987

Richard Cooper, *Gentlemen cricketers of Maldon: two hundred and fifty
   years of cricket in an Essex town.* Oxford Publishing Services 2005

G Cotter, *The Ashes Captains*, Crowood Press 1989

Brian Matthew Crowley and Pat Mullins, *Cradle Days of Australian
   Cricket*, Macmillan Australia 1989

Michael Down, *Archie,* Allen and Unwin 1981

Steven Draper, *Cricket Grounds of Yorkshire*, ACS Publications 1995

L Duckworth, *S.F.Barnes Master Bowler*, Hutchinson 1967

K Dunstan, *The Paddock that grew, the story of Melbourne Cricket Club*,
   Hutchinson, third edition 1988

Jack Egan, *A History of Cricket in Australia*, ABC 1987

Matthew Engel, *Guardian Book of Cricket Pavilions*, Penguin 1988

Robert Allan Fitzgerald, *Wickets in the West* (also known as *The Twelve
   in America)*, Tinsley Brothers 1873

Bill Frindall, *England Test Cricketers – The complete record from 1877*,
   Willow Books, William Collins & Son 1989

W G Grace, *'WG' Cricketing Reminiscences & Personal Recollections*,
   first published 1899, re-printed by Hambledon Press 1980

Eric Greenwood, *A History of East Lancashire Cricket Club
   Part One 1864-1944*, 1999

Gideon Haigh, *Parachutist at fine leg and other unusual occurrences
   from Wisden*, 2007

Chris Harte, *A History of Australian Cricket*, Andre Deutsch 1993

Chris Harte, *The History of South Australian Cricket*, Griffin Press 1990

Basil Haynes and John Lucas, *The Trent Bridge Battery – the Story of the
   Sporting Gunns*, Willow Books 1985

William Henry Hoole, *The Cricketing Squire*,
   Writers' Own Publications 1991

T.P.Horan, *The Australian Tour Team of 1877-79*,
    edited by Frank Tyson, ACS 2001

Pamela Horn, *The Rise and fall of the Victorian Servant*,
    Gill and Macmillan 1975
C.G.Howard, *Lancashire County Cricket – 100 Years of Cricket*,
    Centenary Publications 1964
W.E.Howard, *Fifty years' cricket reminiscences of a non-player*, 1928
John Kay, *A History of County Cricket – Lancashire*, Arthur Barker 1972
A.E.Knight, *The Complete Cricketer*, Methuen and Co 1906
Malcolm Lorimer and Don Ambrose, *Cricket Grounds of Lancashire*,
    ACS Publications 1992
Malcolm Lorimer, *Lancashire County Cricket Club First-Class Records
    1865-1998*, Limlow Books 1999
Roger Luckhurst, *The Mummy's Curse*, Oxford University Press 2012
Mike Marqusee, *Anyone But England – Cricket and the National Malaise*,
    Verso 1994
Christopher Martin-Jenkins, *The Complete Who's Who of Test Cricketers*,
    Hamlyn 1980
Laurence Meynell, *Famous cricket grounds*, Phoenix House 1951
Eric Midwinter, *Red Roses Crest the Caps,* Heinemann Kingswood 1989
Eric Midwinter, *W.G.Grace His life and times*, Allen and Unwin 1981
John Mulvaney and Rex Harcourt, *Aboriginal Tour of 1867-68*,
    Macmillan, revised edition 1988
Charles Pardon, *The Australians in England*, Bell's Life in London, 1882,
    McKenzie 1982
Charles Pardon, *The Australians in England 1884*, Bell's Life in
    London 1884, McKenzie 1984
Tony Percival, *Cheshire Cricketers 1822-1996*, ACS 1997
Jack Pollard, *The Formative years of Australian Cricket 1803-1893*
    Angus Publishers 1987
Edwin Radford, *Encyclopedia of Superstitions*, Philosophical Library 1949
P.E.Reynolds, *The Australian Cricketers Tour of 1878*,
    Mackenzie, reprinted 1980
R Robinson and G Haigh, *On Top Down Under*, Wakefield Press 1975,
    reprinted 1997
Vernon Royle, *Lord Harris's Team in Australia 1878-79; The Diary of
    Vernon Royle*, MCC Cricket Library 2001
A.A.Thomson, *Cricket My Happiness*, Museum Press 1954
Peter Wall, *The life and times of a great Victorian sporting hero –
    Albert Neilson Hornby* (unpublished)
Roy Webber, *The Book of Cricket Records*, Playfair Books 1951
Mark Whitaker, *Running for their Lives*, Yellow Jersey Press 2012
Marcus Williams [ed], *Double Century - 200 Years of Cricket in The Times*,
    Guild Publishing 1985
Anthony Woodhouse, *The History of Yorkshire Cricket*,
    Christopher Helm 1989
Peter Wynne-Thomas, *Cricket Tours – Home and Abroad*, Hamlyn 1989
Peter Wynne-Thomas, Scyld Berry and Cris Freddi, *The Ultimate Cricket
    Fact and Quiz Book*, Stopwatch 1999

Journals and yearbooks
American Cricketer; Cheshire Magazine; Lancashire County Cricket Club 100 years of Cricket - Centenary brochure 1964; *Lancashire Year Books* (various)*; Punch Magazine; The Referee* (magazine, 1915)*; Scores and Biographies* (various)*; Wisden Cricketers' Almanacks* (various)*; The Sporting Mirror* (Volume IV, July to December 1882)

Newspapers
I have consulted the following newspapers: *Manchester Evening News, Manchester Evening Mail, Manchester Guardian, The Times, Stockport Advertiser, Nantwich Chronicle, Liverpool Banner, South Australian Register, Sydney Morning Herald,* Sydney *Morning Telegraph.*

Resources
British Newspaper Library, Colindale, London;
Lancashire C.C.C. library; YouTube.

Websites
Cottontown.org; cricinfo.com [now ESPNcricinfo.com];
cricketarchive.com; lccc.co.uk [Lancashire C.C.C.];
newhumanist.org.uk; normangrubb.co;
pgrfc.co.uk [Preston Grasshoppers]; wikipedia.org

Appendix 1
Career Statistics

Test Cricket: Batting and Fielding

	M	I	NO	R	HS	Av	100	50	ct/st
1878/79	1	2	0	6	4	3.00	-	-	-
1882	1	2	0	11	9	5.50	-	-	-
1884	1	2	0	4	4	2.00	-	-	-
Totals	**3**	**6**	**0**	**21**	**9**	**3.50**	**-**	**-**	**-**

Note: All three of Hornby's Test matches were against Australia. He was bowled four times by F.R.Spofforth and stumped twice by J.M.Blackham.

Test Cricket: Bowling

	O	M	R	W	BB	Av	5wi
1878/79	7	7	0	1	1-0	0.00	-
Totals	**7**	**7**	**0**	**1**	**1-0**	**0.00**	**-**

Note: Hornby's entire Test bowling career comprised seven four-ball maiden overs in Australia's first innings at Melbourne in January 1879, during which he bowled F.E.Allen.

First-Class Cricket: Batting and Fielding

	M	I	NO	R	HS	Av	100	50	ct/st
1867	2	4	0	53	32	13.25	-	-	1
1868	2	4	0	25	9	6.25	-	-	2
1869	5	10	0	203	61	20.30	-	1	2
1870	5	9	1	343	132	42.87	2	-	4
1871	7	13	1	207	75	17.25	-	1	3
1872	7	10	0	314	80	31.40	-	3	9
1873	7	10	0	348	128	34.80	2	1	6
1874	8	15	2	365	72	28.07	-	3	7
1875	13	22	1	646	78*	30.76	-	4	5
1876	19	33	2	965	72	31.12	-	6	13/1
1877	18	29	3	787	144	30.26	2	3	8/1
1878	22	35	0	801	100	22.88	1	3	14
1878/79	5	9	0	167	67	18.55	-	2	2
1879	17	22	2	606	64*	30.30	-	3	13
1880	19	36	3	779	126	23.60	1	3	13
1881	25	38	0	1534	188	40.36	3	7	9
1882	30	53	4	1383	131	28.22	2	7	18
1883	21	36	2	703	96	20.67	-	4	24
1884	18	31	2	678	94	23.37	-	3	13/1
1885	17	29	0	601	84	20.72	-	3	13
1886	20	32	0	842	161	26.31	2	4	12
1887	15	26	1	717	105	28.68	1	4	15
1888	15	27	2	329	50	13.16	-	1	11
1889	18	25	0	433	78	17.32	-	1	10

1890	19	32	2	673	75	22.43	-	4	9
1891	15	23	2	330	57	15.71	-	1	9
1892	9	16	0	210	48	13.12	-	-	3
1893	8	14	1	181	38	13.92	-	-	4
1894	6	9	0	85	44	9.44	-	-	4
1895	8	13	2	196	45*	17.81	-	-	6
1896	6	9	0	116	66	12.88	0	1	12
1897	19	22	6	273	32	17.06	-	-	29
1898	8	10	0	100	27	10.00	-	-	7
1899	3	4	2	116	53	58.00	-	1	3
1906	1	-	-	-	-	-	-	-	-
Totals	**437**	**710**	**41**	**16109**	**188**	**24.07**	**16**	**74**	**313/3**

Notes: Apart from the Australian season of 1878/79, Hornby played all his first-class cricket in England. His last match was for an England XI v West Indians at Blackpool in July 1906, at the age of 59, when because of lumbago he was replaced during the second day by A.E.Peatfield, who batted in both England innings. Hornby was dismissed caught 327 times (49%); 259 times bowled (39%); 38 times lbw (6%); 24 times stumped (4%); 20 times run out (3%); and hit wicket once. He was dismissed most often by W.G.Grace (25 times) and by Alfred Shaw (21 times). For Lancashire he played 292 matches, scoring 10,649 runs at 24.25, including 10 centuries, and taking 215 catches and two stumpings.

First-Class Cricket: Bowling

	O	M	R	W	BB	Av	5wi
1870	12	0	40	4	4-40	10.00	-
1872	3	0	8	0	-	-	-
1875	7	1	20	0	-	-	-
1878	5	2	5	1	1-2	5.00	-
1878/79	79	48	79	4	2-9	19.75	-
1879	2	1	1	0	-	-	-
1880	22	10	27	1	1-2	27.00	-
1881	4	0	11	1	1-7	11.00	-
1882	5	0	28	0	-	-	-
1883	1	0	6	0	-	-	-
1884	4	0	11	0	-	-	-
1885	2	0	10	0	-	-	-
1888	1	0	4	0	-	-	-
1899	1	0	8	0	-	-	-
Totals	**147**	**62**	**258**	**11**	**4-40**	**23.45**	**-**

Notes: Hornby bowled in 27 of his 437 first-class matches; his overs were of four balls throughout his career apart from a single five-ball over in 1899. He took wickets at the rate of one per 53.90 balls and conceded runs at a rate equivalent to 2.61 per six-ball over. Five of his eleven wickets were bowled, five caught and one stumped. His best bowling return was four for 40 off twelve four-ball overs, with no maidens, for Gentlemen of the North in the first innings of Gentlemen of the South at Beeston in August 1870, the first time he had bowled in first-class cricket. For Lancashire he took, in all, three wickets for 94.

First-Class Cricket: Centuries (16)

Score	For	Opponent	Venue	Season
132	Lancashire[1]	Hampshire	Old Trafford	1870
103	Gentlemen of North[1]	Gentlemen of South	Beeston	1870
128	Lancashire[1]	Surrey	Old Trafford	1873

104	Gentlemen[1]	Players	Prince's	1873
144	Gentlemen[1]	Players	The Oval	1877
105	England[1]	Gloucs & Yorkshire	Lord's	1877
100	Lancashire[2]	Gloucestershire	Old Trafford	1878
126	Lancashire[2]	Surrey	The Oval	1880
188	Lancashire[1]	Derbyshire	Old Trafford	1881
102	Lancashire[1]	Kent	Old Trafford	1881
145	Lancashire[1]	Derbyshire	Derby	1881
121*	MCC[2]	Cambridge Univ	Lord's	1882
131	Lancashire[1]	Middlesex	Lord's	1882
111	Lancashire[1]	Oxford Univ	Old Trafford	1886
161	Lancashire[1]	Surrey	Liverpool	1886
105	MCC[1]	Kent	Lord's	1887

Note: The index figures [1] and [2] above indicate the innings in which the feat was achieved.

Edward Kenworthy and Cecil Lumsden Hornby

Two of Albert Hornby's older brothers played briefly in first-class cricket. E.K., born in 1839, played one match for Gentlemen of the North at Beeston in 1862, scoring 31 in his only innings and taking one catch. C.L., born in 1843, played in two matches, one for the Gentlemen of England in 1874 and one for Lancashire in 1877. In these, he scored 27 runs at 9.00, took one for 3 in two four-ball overs and held no catches.

Sources for all the above: www. cricketarchive.com and Wisden Cricketers' Almanack.

Appendix 2

Hornby's last Championship match

LEICESTERSHIRE v LANCASHIRE
Played at Grace Road, Leicester, July 10, 11, 12, 1899.

Leicestershire won the toss and decided to bat

Leicestershire innings

*CE de Trafford	c Webb b Hallows	75	c AH Hornby b Sharp	14
AE Knight	c AN Hornby b Webb	82	b Mold	38
AD Pougher	b Cuttell	67	b Sharp	2
R Joyce	b Webb	1	lbw b Webb	9
JH King	c AN Hornby b Sharp	31	c Tyldesley b Mold	12
JH Brown	b Cuttell	3	b Sharp	30
H Whitehead	b Cuttell	6	b Mold	0
F Geeson	c Smith b Cuttell	5	b Hallows	14
C Agar	run out	0	b Mold	4
+JP Whiteside	not out	0	not out	1
G Grewcock	b Cuttell	0	b Mold	1
Extras	(6 b, 3 lb, 1 nb, 1 w)	11	(13 b, 1 lb)	14
Total	**(all out, 132 overs)**	**281**	**(all out, 88 overs)**	**139**

FoW (1): 1-104, 2-222, 3-226, 4-236, 5-262, 6-276, 7-276, 8-281, 9-281,
10-281 (132 ov)
FoW (2): 1-21, 2-25, 3-52, 4-81, 5-86, 6-86, 7-111, 8-124, 9-136, 10-139 (88 ov)

Lancashire first innings

CR Hartley	c and b Geeson	32
AH Hornby	b Geeson	18
JT Tyldesley	c Brown b Whitehead	249
WR Cuttell	b Grewcock	44
A Eccles	b King	30
J Sharp	b Joyce	72
J Hallows	c sub b Grewcock	60
+C Smith	b Geeson	10
*AN Hornby	c Grewcock b Agar	53
S Webb	not out	8
AW Mold	c Geeson b Agar	3
Extras	(4 b, 4 lb, 1 nb, 2 w)	11
Total	**(all out, 174 overs)**	**590**

FoW (1): 1-41, 2-50, 3-159, 4-224, 5-371, 6-510, 7-510, 8-573, 9-579,
10-590 (174 ov)

Lancashire bowling

	O	M	R	W		O	M	R	W
Cuttell	49	26	74	5		23	12	27	0
Webb	21	6	51	2		19	12	13	1
Mold	16	3	40	0		16	8	24	5
Sharp	26	10	53	1		21	7	41	3
Hallows	16	4	35	1		9	2	20	1
Tyldesley	3	0	9	0					
AN Hornby	1	0	8	0					

Leicestershire bowling

	O	M	R	W
Geeson	29	6	79	3
Grewcock	38	6	118	2
Agar	38	7	132	2
King	32	10	90	1
Brown	16	2	59	0
Pougher	5	0	28	0
Joyce	9	0	49	1
Whitehead	7	2	24	1

Umpires: J Moss, JJ Tuck
Close of play day 1: Leicestershire (1) 281 all out
Close of play day 2: Lancashire 554/7 (Smith 4*, AN Hornby 39*)

Lancashire won by an innings and 170 runs.

Source: cricketarchive.com

Such a heavy defeat for Leicestershire, after they were at one stage 222 for 1, represents one of the greatest turn-rounds in cricket history. For Hornby, who scored a run for every year of his age and had his son playing alongside him, it couldn't get much better and he promptly retired.

Index

A page number in bold indicates an illustration.